# 50 HANDS-ON ADVANCED LITERACY STRATEGIES for Young Learners

PreK–Grade 2

*50 Hands-On Advanced Literacy Strategies for Young Learners, PreK-Grade 2* is your go-to resource for lessons, strategies, and activities to foster the key skills and thinking strategies needed to excel in literacy.

The hands-on, minds-on literacy explorations in this book are designed to feel a lot like play, but are rooted in the foundational literacy practices that all young learners need. Packed with engaging and helpful reproducibles, each activity is thoughtfully laid out with skill(s), materials, introduction, hands-on task, and reflection sections to maximize student learning. Instructions on how to scaffold experiences for a wider range of ages and developmental readiness levels makes this resource eminently flexible.

Ideal for learners in grades PreK–2, this book is for teachers, curriculum coaches, parents, librarians, and community educators looking to work on target literacy skills.

**Allison Bemiss** has worked to encourage critical and creative thinking in early childhood and elementary-age children for nearly 20 years, while serving as a teacher, interventionist, and education consultant. She currently works for a local educational cooperative developing and leading workshops in the areas of literacy, STE(A)M, and family engagement.

# 50 HANDS-ON ADVANCED LITERACY STRATEGIES for Young Learners

PreK–Grade 2

Allison Bemiss

Routledge
Taylor & Francis Group
NEW YORK AND LONDON

Prufrock Press Inc.
P.O. Box 8813
Waco, TX 76714-8813
Phone: (800) 998-2208
Fax: (800) 240-0333
http://www.prufrock.com

Cover image: © Getty Images

First published 2023
by Routledge
605 Third Avenue, New York NY 10158

and by Routledge
4 Park Square, Milton Park, Abingdon, Oxon OX14 4RN

*Routledge is an imprint of the Taylor & Francis Group, an informa business*

© 2023 Taylor & Francis

The right of Allison Bemiss to be identified as author of this work has been asserted in accordance with sections 77 and 78 of the Copyright, Designs and Patents Act 1988.

All rights reserved. The purchase of this copyright material confers the right on the purchasing institution to photocopy pages which bear the copyright line at the bottom of the page. No other parts of this book may be reprinted or reproduced or utilised in any form or by any electronic, mechanical, or other means, now known or hereafter invented, including photocopying and recording, or in any information storage or retrieval system, without permission in writing from the publishers.

Trademark notice: Product or corporate names may be trademarks or registered trademarks, and are used only for identification and explanation without intent to infringe.

*Library of Congress Cataloging-in-Publication Data*
Names: Bemiss, Allison, author.
Title: 50 hands-on advanced literacy strategies for young learners, preK-grade 2 / Allison Bemiss.
Other titles: Fifty hands-on advanced literacy strategies for young learners, preK-grade 2
Description: New York, NY : Routledge, 2023. | Includes bibliographical references. |
Identifiers: LCCN 2022007851 (print) | LCCN 2022007852 (ebook) |
    ISBN 9781032307800 (hardback) | ISBN 9781032307466 (paperback) |
    ISBN 9781003306627 (ebook)
Subjects: LCSH: Language arts (Early childhood) | Language arts (Elementary) |
    Creative activities and seat work. | Early childhood education—Activity programs. |
    Education, Elementary—Activity programs.
Classification: LCC LB1139.5.L35 B45 2023 (print) | LCC LB1139.5.L35 (ebook) |
    DDC 372.6/044—dc23
LC record available at https://lccn.loc.gov/2022007851
LC ebook record available at https://lccn.loc.gov/2022007852

ISBN: 978-1-032-30780-0 (hbk)
ISBN: 978-1-032-30746-6 (pbk)
ISBN: 978-1-003-30662-7 (ebk)

DOI: 10.4324/9781003306627

Typeset in Warnock Pro
by Apex CoVantage, LLC

# Contents

Introduction ... 1

## PART 1
### Hands-On Word Recognition

1. Code-a-Bracelet (segmenting/blending: word in a sentence or phonemes) ... 12
2. Rhyming Hot Potato (rhyming) ... 13
3. Sloth Talk (segmenting/blending: onset and rime and phonemes) ... 16
4. Decoding Bowling (blending onset and rime or digraphs) ... 20
5. The Floor Is Lava (blending onset and rime or split digraph/magic e) ... 22
6. Seek and Find (segmenting: syllables or phonemes) ... 23
7. Snowman Spy (phoneme isolation) ... 25
8. Wizard Words (phoneme isolation: ending sounds or long vowel sounds) ... 30
9. Silly Animal Sounds (deleting phonemes) ... 33
10. Syllable Surgery (segmenting syllables or sorting open/closed syllables) ... 36
11. Backwards Day Hopscotch (reversal: compound words or phonemes) ... 39
12. Feed the Monster (phoneme isolation or phoneme reversal) ... 44
13. Buried Treasure (consonant blends:r or r controlled vowel:ar) ... 49
14. Wild Sounds Safari (consonant blends: beginning or ending sounds) ... 53
15. Letter Teams (consonant digraphs or unpredictable vowel team:ea) ... 56
16. Mirror Mirror (blends or diphthongs) ... 60

# Contents

| | | |
|---|---|---|
| 17 | Building Words (substituting/blending: compound words or phonemes) | 64 |
| 18 | Fairy Tale Forest Map (substituting phonemes) | 67 |
| 19 | Say It, Create It (mapping words) | 73 |
| 20 | Dramatic Dominos (fluency) | 76 |

## PART 2
### Hands-On Language Comprehension

| | | |
|---|---|---|
| 21 | Ca-TOWER-Gories: Building Vocabulary (vocabulary: categories) | 82 |
| 22 | Jack In the Box (vocabulary) | 85 |
| 23 | Word Mural (semantics/visualizing vocabulary) | 86 |
| 24 | Homophone Hockey (homophones) | 88 |
| 25 | Synonym Splash (synonyms) | 90 |
| 26 | ANTonyms In the Pants (antonyms) | 92 |
| 27 | Mystery Box (synonyms/antonyms) | 96 |
| 28 | Don't Spill the Beans (idioms) | 99 |
| 29 | Morphology Tree (morphemes: prefixes, suffixes, and base words) | 103 |
| 30 | Syntax Salad (syntax) | 106 |
| 31 | Prag-Meme-Tic (pragmatics) | 110 |
| 32 | Snack Time Sequencing (sequencing) | 114 |
| 33 | Graffiti Road (sequencing/retelling or summarizing) | 117 |
| 34 | Never Be a Know It All (questioning for understanding) | 120 |
| 35 | Beach Ball Book Club (questioning for discussion) | 123 |
| 36 | Class Connection Chain (making connections) | 124 |
| 37 | Top Secret: Character Feelings Challenge (making inferences) | 126 |
| 38 | Character Inside and Out (character traits/analysis) | 129 |
| 39 | Story Glove (characteristics of fiction: story elements) | 132 |
| 40 | Wild About Text Features (characteristics of nonfiction: text features) | 135 |

## PART 3
### Hands-On Writing

| | | |
|---|---|---|
| 41 | Share Bear: Be a Storyteller (storytelling and idea development) | 142 |
| 42 | Beary Delicious Details (descriptive writing: sensory details and/or figurative language) | 145 |

## Contents

| | | |
|---|---|---|
| 43 | Number Narrative (narrative) | 148 |
| 44 | Mystery Text (narrative) | 149 |
| 45 | Would You Rather? (persuasive) | 153 |
| 46 | Shadow Zoo (expository) | 157 |
| 47 | Snowman STEAM: How To (expository) | 161 |
| 48 | Lights, Camera, Action! (types of sentence/writing convention/fluency) | 165 |
| 49 | Genie Writing Wishes (revision and peer conference) | 168 |
| 50 | Editor Spinner (editing) | 171 |

# Introduction

"Play is the work of the child." These infamous words shared by Maria Montessori are at the heart of what early childhood (birth to age 8) educators and caregivers see every day as they explore alongside children. Play-based learning has become a buzzword in education, and for a good reason. Young children not only explore the world around them through play, but they also process current understandings and feelings through it. Social skills, problem solving, self-regulation, and content exploration are all explored through four little letters – P-L-A-Y. I think most early childhood folks agree that children need time during the day that is specifically devoted to free play for each of these reasons and more.

While one of our jobs as early childhood educators is to protect and support this play experience, we also have a responsibility to provide developmentally appropriate structured practices to engage young learners in explorations that build the foundation for the rest of their education. One way to do this is to harness the high level of engagement that originates from play and use it as a hook for the content, thinking strategies, and new schema we want children to build and explore. Hands-on, minds-on opportunities rooted in play, paired with instruction founded in research and evidence-based practices, offer a wonderful way to engage students in meaningful yet developmentally appropriate practices. This is true for any content area or domain, including literacy.

DOI: 10.4324/9781003306627-1

# Introduction

## What Does It Mean to Engage Young Learners in Literacy?

Reading is often the first word that comes to mind when folks think of literacy. "Read" is such a simple word for so many larger skills and experiences. How to best teach reading has been the subject of debate for a number of years. *A Simple View of Reading* is a theory developed in 1986 by Philip Gough and William Tunmer. It is expressed as *decoding (D) x language comprehension (LC) = reading comprehension (RC)*. Gough and Tunmer, two psychologists, developed this formula as a way to explain how word recognition or decoding strategies and comprehension skills work together to form the foundation for reading comprehension. In 2001, Dr. Hollis Scarborough, a leading researcher in early literacy, published the *Reading Rope* infographic seen in Figure I.1. Dr. Scarborough's Reading Rope delves further into explaining how each of the strands of literacy found within word recognition and language comprehension build a child's foundation for reading comprehension (Scarborough, 2001).

While reading is one important component of literacy, it certainly isn't the only one. A child's curriculum should offer opportunities to explore all

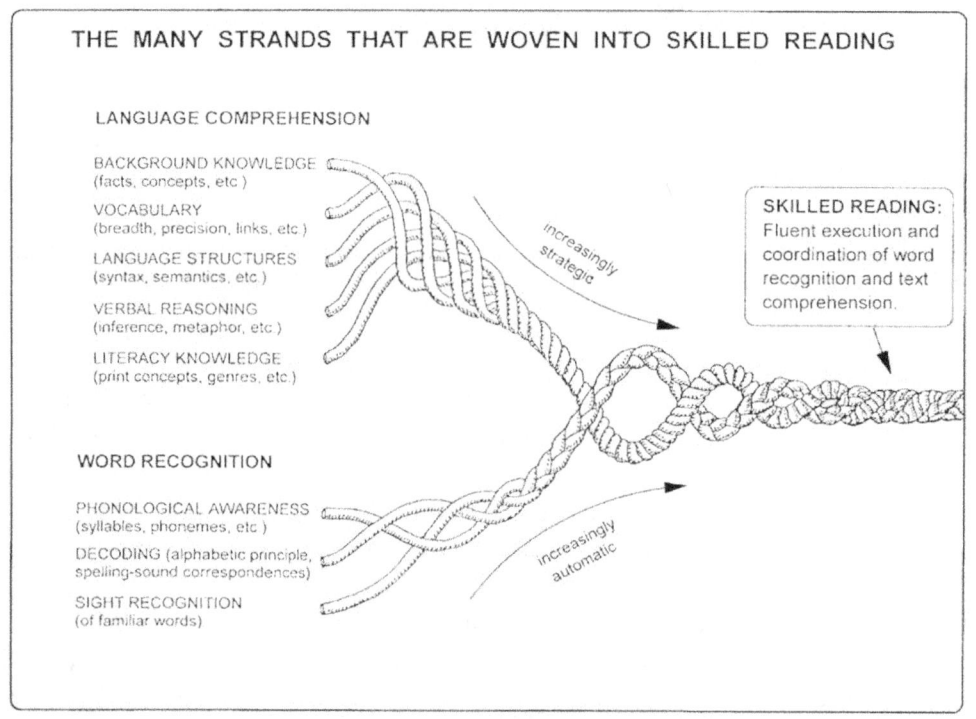

**Figure I.1**

four areas of literacy, including listening, speaking, writing, *and* reading. The beauty of incorporating hands-on, minds-on instruction into your literacy curriculum is that it will offer diverse, meaningful, and authentic opportunities for students to engage in listening and speaking as they explore reading and writing's foundational skills.

In this book, you'll find 50 literacy activities to strengthen or expand your young learners' foundational literacy skills (reading, writing, speaking, and listening) on the following topics:

- word recognition (i.e., phonological awareness, phonics, fluency)
- comprehension (i.e., morphology, semantics, critical thinking strategies)
- writing (i.e., idea development, drafting, editing, revising).

## Small Groups: Big Benefits

Small groups can be a powerful time to work with learners of all levels of readiness. While educators quickly recognize that small groups are beneficial for learners with a lower level of readiness in a topic, small groups are a powerhouse teaching tool for *all* students. Each child in our room deserves focused and meaningful instruction around important skills.

For this reason, most of the mini-lessons in this text are suggested for use in small group instruction. Although that certainly isn't the only way to utilize these experiences, I would encourage you to give it a try! While this book is targeted at advanced young learners, it would be foolish to believe that means each of your advanced learners will be innately curious or precocious in exactly the same areas of literacy. One child may excel in phonemic awareness or phonics, but another is excellent at critical thinking skills and vocabulary. Each child's interests and readiness levels will be as inherently unique as the child. Small groups are a wonderful way of engaging and getting to know your students. It also offers an opportunity to personalize experiences, questioning, and scaffold tasks to meet the unique readiness levels of your young learners.

Small group time researchers Robert Marzano and John Hattie agree that cooperative learning is only effective when you

- structure it carefully
- keep groups small
- teach students how to work in groups.

These prominent researchers continue to translate evidence-based practices for educators as they review the effect sizes of mega research studies to assemble a list of high yield practices (Hattie and Marzano, 2021). All eight of the following practices are further translated into what it can look like in preK-2 classrooms through the routines, protocols, and structures provided in the tasks in this book:

1. Ensure a Clear Focus for the Lesson.
2. Offer Overt Instruction.
3. Get the Students to Engage with the Content.
4. Give Feedback.
5. Provide numerous Exposures.
6. Have Students Apply Their Knowledge.
7. Get Students Working Together.
8. Build Students' Self-Efficacy.

Small group instruction is also the perfect time to listen to your children, hear their thinking as they puzzle out problems, and make notes to guide differentiation.

## There's a Big Difference Between a 3-Year-Old and a 7- or 8-Year-Old. How Can These Experiences Work for Such a Wide Range of Learners?

If you are asking yourself this question, you are not alone! I pondered, explored, and tested these tasks with children of all ages in a variety of settings, along with some help from a group of fantastic educators. The first thing I did to help with this concern was to divide skills, strategies, or scaffolds within the task instructions into two levels:

- ❏ little literacy learners
- ❏ leveled-up literacy learners

As an advocate for precocious youth, I feel it is advantageous to our young learners not to delineate these two levels with ages. Yes, typically speaking, your little lit learners will be younger children, and leveled-up lit learners will be older children; however, this is not always going to be the case. Each simply offers two variations for the activity. In one task, blends may be addressed for the little lit version, but in another task, blends may be addressed in a different way for the leveled-up lit version. I strongly encourage you to look at the *specific skill* you are teaching in that experience and match it to the child's current needs and understandings. Depending on their schema, children may move back and forth between these two levels as they focus on different skills and strategies.

If you've read my other books or are friends on social media, you may know that I'm the parent of an exceptionally curious and unique little learner who is also a stroke survivor with multiple diagnoses, including autism and cerebral palsy. I have always been a strong and devoted advocate for open tasks and universal design for learning for all learners, including those who are gifted, precocious, or twice-exceptional. Several of the language comprehension and writing tasks in this book are open tasks, meaning that students will work on the same strategy or target skill; however, the child will work to complete the task using their own current readiness level and schema as a guide, while exploring the concept. This is explained in greater detail in each task. These explorations also share suggested structures and scaffolds to support the youngest little literacy learners or tips for supporting leveled-up literacy learners with additional ideas for extensions to provide additional challenge opportunities.

If you are a gifted education (or talent development) teacher reading this, you will use these levels to pick and choose options to tailor the experience to match the needs of your students. If you are a classroom teacher working with a variety of levels, you will also do this; however, you may find that you are able to use both versions of the task with different students in your classroom. An example of this can be seen in the task in the language comprehension section called "Synonym Splash." The little lit version of the task requires students to match synonyms, while the leveled-up version requires students to practice generating synonyms. This simple but powerful change offers students a way to explore a similar skill at a scaffolded level of challenge to reflect their needs. The beauty of this type of personalization is that to the average onlooker, it would appear students are completing the same engaging lessons. They are both "playing" with rubber duckies and exploring synonyms, yet the experience is actually differentiated. This is my favorite way to personalize learning through universal design.

Last, the terms little literacy learning and leveled-up literacy learning are meant for teacher use. A child does not need to know they are being called back to a higher or lower level of the task. These terms are provided to help you plan, prepare, and proactively meet the needs of your little ones. They are not intended for student use as an identifiable group name.

## How Do I Group Students?

Vary it. Is it good to group all of your students with a higher level of readiness together? Yes. But I say that with a very important caveat. You should be looking at data related to specific targeted skills. As you form groups, looking at overall literacy skills (or reading levels) is not the most effective way to do this. For example, you may have a child who is off the charts in vocabulary but struggles with phonics and decoding. The experiences you provide your students need to match their individual readiness levels in the subsets of each skill. It is also important that you do not group students based on readiness levels alone. Sometimes you should group students by interests or preferred learning environments. The most important thing here is to vary your grouping methods and do it with purpose.

## How Are These Experiences Structured?

Each of the tasks will have a one-page activity description. With the exception of a handful of lessons (primarily the writing tasks that include time for idea development and writing), these lessons are planned for a quick mini-lesson to review or introduce content students have previously explored in their core curriculum. These introductions generally take around 5–10 minutes, time for students to work in a small group with you, peer groups, or pairs to delve deeply into the hands-on task. This will typically take around 15 minutes. Finally, the lesson offers a quick reflection or discussion question that can be used as a part of a think pair share or even a "Ticket Out the Door" if you are closing out the activity at a time of transition. These timelines are a fluid suggestion. Actual time will vary depending on the age and developmental readiness levels of your students. As with everything else suggested in this book, you are the advocate for your students' individual needs. Please modify, adapt, and personalize this curriculum to match the needs of your students.

Each experience is written in the following format:

- ❏ Skill(s): Focus for little literacy and leveled-up literacy learners.
- ❏ Materials: Materials needed per class, small group, or student.
- ❏ Introduction: The teachers will introduce or review a strategy. Then model the task students will complete.
- ❏ Hands-On Task: The students will create, practice, or explore a specific skill in an engaging hands-on manner alongside the teacher, small group, or in pairs.
- ❏ Reflection: A discussion prompt to help students extend and apply their understanding of the targeted skill.

## References

Gough, P. and Tunmer, W. (1986). Decoding, reading, and reading disability. *Remedial and Special Education, 7,* 6–10.

Hattie, J. and Marzano, R. (2012). *8 strategies Robert Marzano & John Hattie agree on,* September 27. Evidence-Based Teaching. http://www.evidencebasedteaching.org.au/robert-marzano-vs-john-hattie/

Montessori, Maria. (2019). *Play is the work of the child,* July 23. Child Development Institute. https://childdevelopmentinfo.com/child-development/play-work-of-children/#gs.nu0nja

Scarborough, H. S. (2001). Connecting early language and literacy to later reading (dis)abilities: Evidence, theory, and practice. In S. Neuman & D. Dickinson (eds.), *Handbook for research in early literacy* (pp. 97–110). New York: Guilford Press.

# PART 1

# Hands-On Word Recognition

Word recognition encompasses a multitude of skills that provide an important block in the foundation of skilled reading. In the Reading Rope shared in the Introduction (Figure I.1), phonological awareness, decoding, and sight recognition are recognized as the three categories for word recognition. The hands-on, minds-on experiences shared in this part focus on skills within these three areas. The *little literacy learners* version of each of these tasks will focus primarily on phonological awareness and decoding with an emphasis on building letter-sound connections. The *leveled-up literacy learners* version focuses on the more advanced skills in phonological and phonemic awareness, decoding, and sight words.

Turn on your favorite song. Now close your eyes and listen to the lyrics, clapping to the beat of each verse or word. Now, listen to the chorus again. Do you notice any words that rhyme? This is a part of phonological awareness, and it can be done with your eyes closed. Phonological awareness is the ability to notice, find patterns, and manipulate sounds in spoken language. It is the foundation for which all other literacy skills are built and begins long before the child learns their first letter name. Phonological awareness skills usually develop in a predictable order beginning with word awareness in sentences, recognizing rhyme or alliteration, segmenting words into syllables, and noticing patterns with onset and rime that will then allow them to generate their own rhymes. Phonological awareness is a larger umbrella term that also encompasses phonemic awareness. Phonemic awareness includes the more advanced phonological skills, such as noticing the individual phonemes, or sounds, within words. Students may count these sounds and manipulate them by segmenting or blending them. Finally, students will be ready to swap, delete, or reverse phonemes. When working in phonological awareness in a small group or if students will be working independently, it is often necessary to have a visual model since they are working with the spoken language or sounds. Children will need to move from concrete to abstract as they explore these word recognition strategies (Figure 1.1).

If students are just beginning to explore a skill, it is best to gather a collection of actual objects rather than using printable pictures. If students are

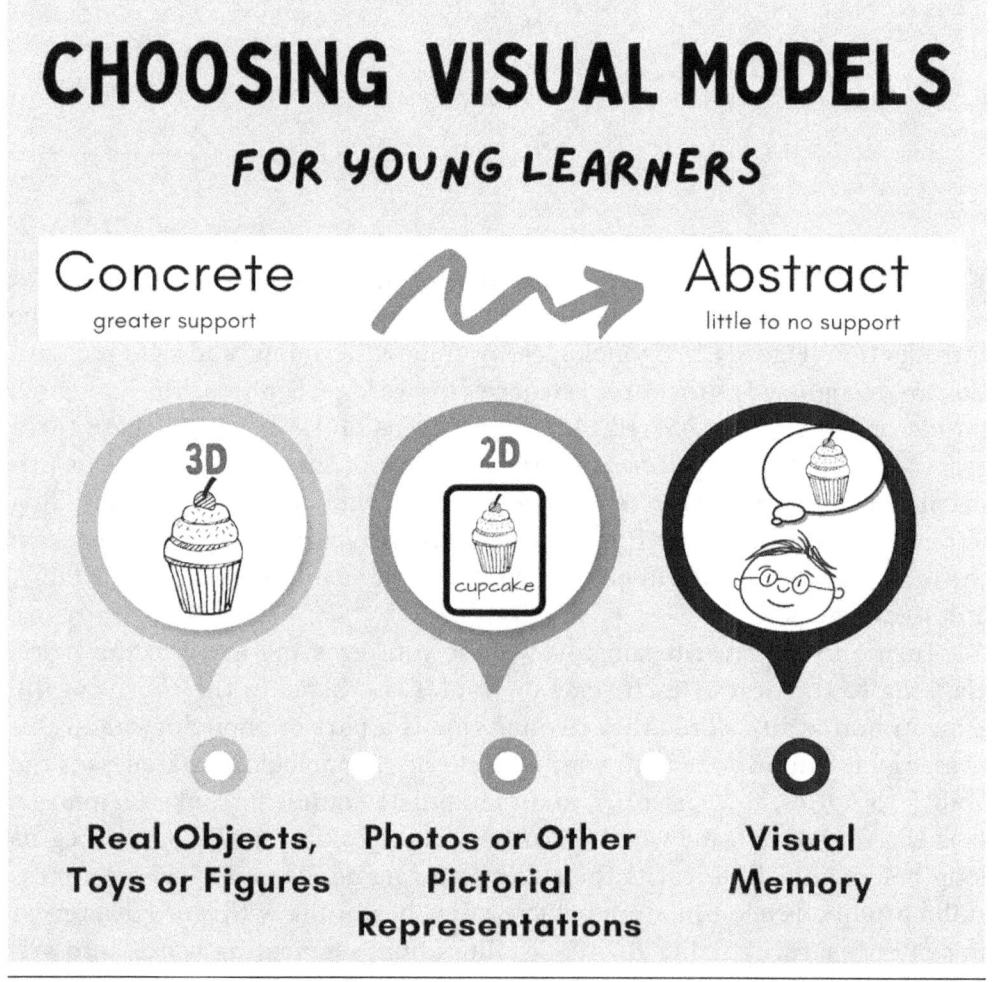

Figure 1.1

more advanced with a skill, you can increase the challenge by using photos or other pictorial representations such as blackline drawings. The greatest level of challenge would be to ask students to visualize the word from memory without an object or pictorial representation. Picture cards, drawings, or blackline picture representations are included in many of the tasks; however, if students are just beginning to explore the skill or strategy, consider collecting objects or trinkets (toys) of objects students can use for these tasks in lieu of picture cards.

Phonological awareness skills begin in infancy as children listen to their parents sing and continue to develop through nursery rhymes and play in the early childhood years, but it doesn't end there. Early in my teaching career, I made the unfortunate mistake of thinking that, once children were readers, they needed to spend all their time on phonics or comprehension, often neglecting the more advanced phonemic awareness skills like swapping, deleting, or reversing phonemes.

Taking time to explore and develop a deeper understanding of phonemes helps strengthen the next component of the Reading Rope, decoding. Decoding or phonics is the ability to make sound-letter connections and apply relationships and patterns as they explore new words. It is imperative that students have a strong phonological awareness and, more specifically, phonemic awareness background to aid them in decoding words (Gough and Tunmer, 1986).

Fantastic. Terrible. Boisterous. Were you able to read all three of those words without sounding them out? If so, they are sight words for you! A sight word is a word that you can read without sounding it out. If you provide children with strong phonological awareness skills, including the more advanced skills of deleting and adding phonemes to words, many of the high frequency words will be decodable. While the reading rope specifically discusses decoding, it's also important to consider encoding or orthographic mapping as a process to help children learn new words. The task in this chapter, "Say It, Create It," is an example of this strategy. This process is helpful for irregular sight words (e.g., in "said," *ai* makes the /e/ sound, s-ai-d). As students use encoding to explore irregular words, they can note the irregular word pattern as they write the word. Teachers have found success with the Heart Word Model for this skill by asking students to draw a heart around the irregular pattern (i.e., *ai*) as they map and write the word during this encoding process (Farrell, Hunter, and Osenga, 2020).

Word recognition is a critical component in developing skilled readers and is sometimes left out for children who are early readers. The word recognition lessons in this book are f-u-n, hands-on, and minds-on opportunities to strengthen these skills.

# 50 HANDS-ON ADVANCED Literacy Strategies

## 1 Code-a-Bracelet

### Skill

- Little lit learners: Segmenting/blending words in sentences.
- Leveled-up lit learners: Segmenting/blending phonemes.

### Materials per Child

- Pipe cleaner
- Pony beads

### Introduction

In this exploration, children will learn something new about a friend (bracelet buddy) and use the information to code a friendship bracelet. Little lit learners will explore segmenting a sentence into words using a bead to represent each word in a sentence their bracelet buddy shares. Leveled-up lit learners will code the individual phonemes in the word that their bracelet buddy shares. Model this activity by inviting a child to come up and work with you as your "bracelet buddy." You will create a friendship bracelet based on your buddy's answers, and he will do the same for you. Model thinking aloud as you code your friendship bracelet.

### Hands-On Literacy Task

### Little Lit Learners

1. Students will work in pairs/bracelet buddies. The first child will share the answer to this sentence starter. "A friend is _____." (i.e., kind, fun, nice, helpful)
2. Bracelet buddies will work together to segment the sentence into words by adding one bead to the bracelet for each word. (4 beads: a friend is kind)
3. Bracelet buddies will complete the same steps to create the second child's bracelet.

### Leveled-Up Lit Learners

1. Students will work in pairs/bracelet buddies. The first child will share a personal characteristic that makes them a good friend. (i.e., silly, forgiving)

# Part 1 Hands-On Word Recognition

2 Bracelet buddies will work together to segment this word into phonemes by adding one bead to the bracelet for each sound in the word. (4 beads: k-i-n-d)
3 Bracelet buddies will complete the same steps to create the second child's bracelet.

## *Whole Group or Small Group Reflection Prompt*

"What is another sentence [little lit] or word [leveled-up] that would match the number of beads on your friendship bracelet?"

## 2 Rhyming Hot Potato

**Figure 1.2**

# 50 HANDS-ON ADVANCED Literacy Strategies

### *Skill*

- ❏ Little lit learners: Rhyming.
- ❏ Leveled-up lit learners: Rhyming.

### Materials per Group

- ❏ Hot potato (a small potato or create one by stuffing a brown sock with cotton or paper)
- ❏ Syllable dice [leveled-up lit learners]

### Introduction

Show students the "hot potato." Tell students today you will play the game by saying a rhyming word each time you toss the potato to a friend. For the little lit learners version, give them an "at" pattern word to begin the task. For the leveled-up version, roll the syllable dice and brainstorm a word with the same number of syllables. Ask students to think of a word that rhymes with your word. Now show them how to rhyme using a nonsensical word (i.e., birthday: smirthday, kirthday). Students can play the game using real or nonsensical words. For very young little lit learners, consider having a selection of small objects or photos with the "at" pattern. This will provide a scaffold to help them generate rhymes.

### Hands-On Literacy Task

1. Children take turns generating rhymes using the original word while tossing the hot potato back and forth.
2. The child without the hot potato at the end of 45 seconds is the champion and will get to brainstorm the starting word for the next round for their group.
3. Continue this pattern for as many rounds as you have time for during your lesson.

### Whole Group or Small Group Reflection Prompt

"I wonder how practicing rhyming words could help us learn to say, read, or write new words."

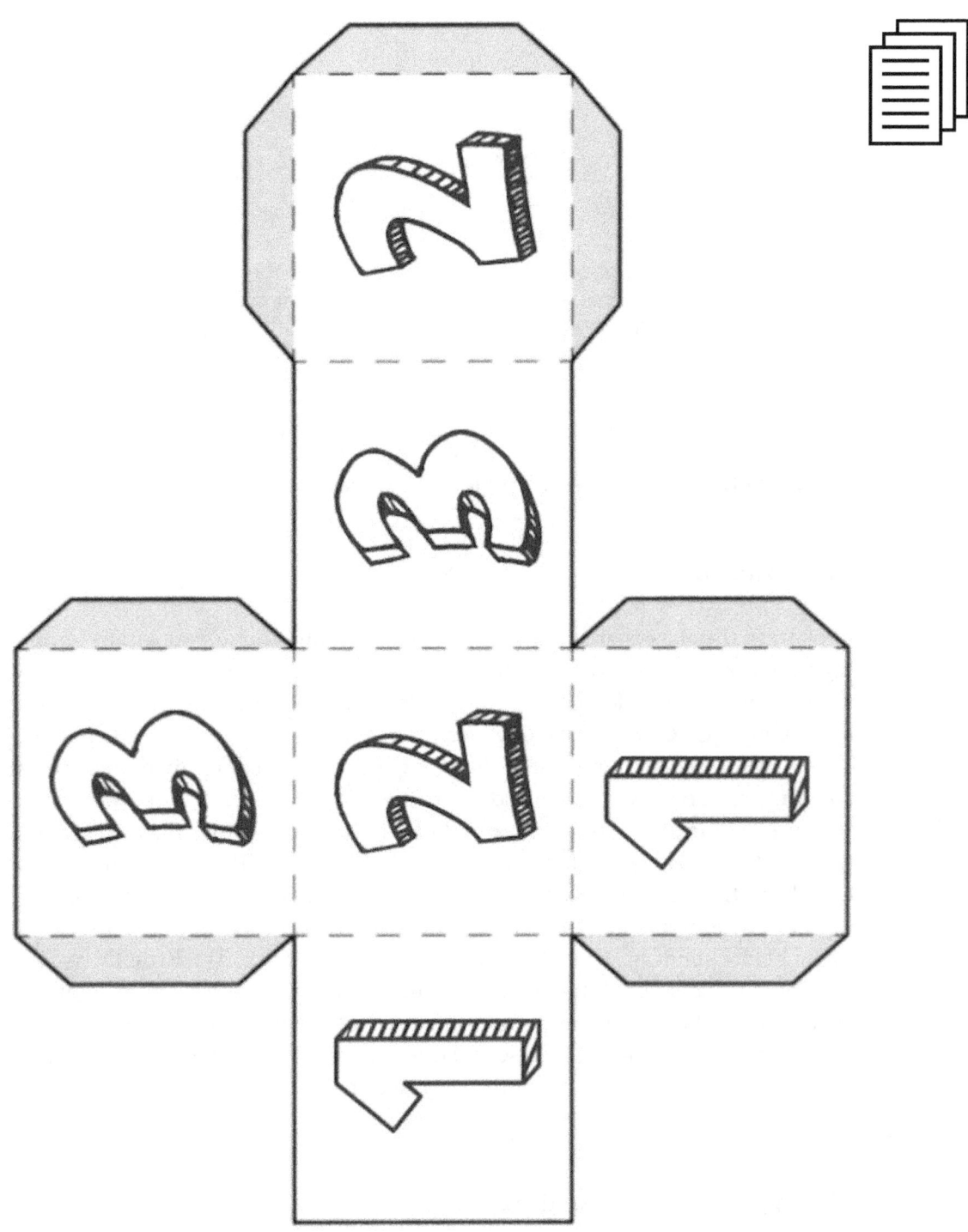

**Blackline Master 1.1**

© Allison Bemiss, *50 Hands-On Advanced Literacy Strategies for Young Learners, PreK–Grade 2*. Routledge 2023

# 50 HANDS-ON ADVANCED Literacy Strategies

## 3 Sloth Talk

### Skill

- ❏ Little lit learners: Segmenting/blending phonemes.
- ❏ Leveled-up lit learners: Segmenting/blending phonemes.

### Materials per Pair

- ❏ Picture cards [little lit and leveled-up versions]

### Introduction

Explain to the class that sloths move very slowly, and today, you will be speaking slowly in the same way a sloth moves. In order to speak like a sloth, you say each sound of a word for 1 or 2 seconds. Practice "sloth talk" with the students using simple CVC words like dog: d-o-g or rat: r-a-t. Next, model the partner game for the class. Invite a student to be your partner for this model. Draw a picture card from a stack, but do not show your partner. Say the word very slowly, isolating each sound. (i.e., c-a-t) Repeat the word using "sloth talk" a few times, inviting your partner to say the sounds with you. Then ask your partner to tell you the word she heard. Show the class or small group the picture card to determine if your partner got the word correct. Practice this game a few times before sending students to play sloth talk in pairs. The little lit version uses the first set of sloth talk picture cards. For the youngest learners, you can adapt this further by having students blend or segment onset and rime (i.e., cat: c-at) rather than blending each sound individually. The leveled-up literacy version uses the second set of picture cards that include words with four or more phonemes.

### Hands-On Literacy Task

1. Students will work in pairs. They will have a deck of picture cards flipped upside down in between them.
2. Partner 1 will look at the picture card and say the word slowly, segmenting each phoneme using "sloth talk." Repeating it a few times, inviting their partner to repeat the sounds with them on the second or third repetition.

3. Partner 2 will call out the word they hear and check it using the picture card.
4. The partners will switch roles and play the game again.
5. Continue this pattern for as many rounds as you have time for during your lesson.

## Whole Group or Small Group Reflection Prompt

"I noticed we could really hear the sounds in the words when our partners said them slowly like a sloth. How could listening to sounds while using sloth talk help us become better speakers or readers?"

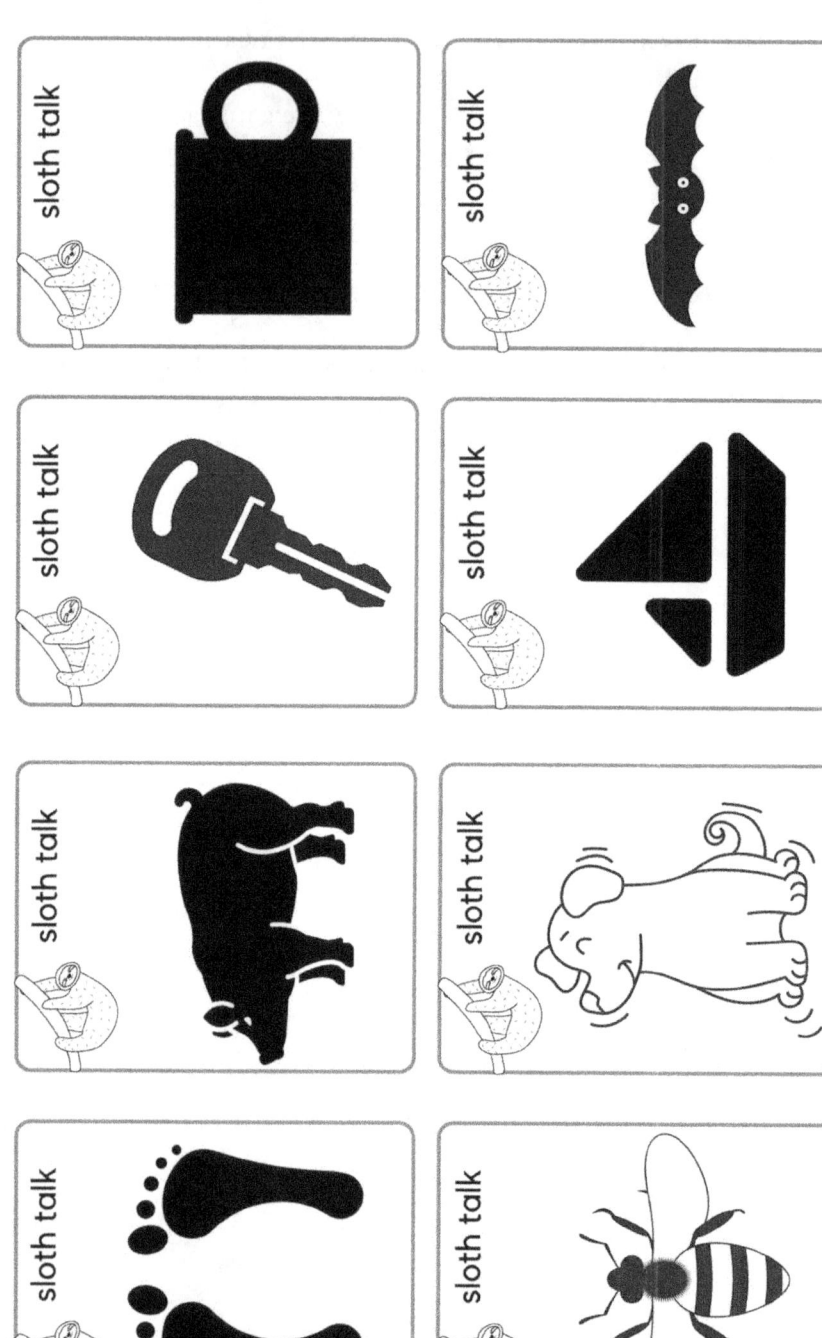

# Leveled-Up Literacy Learners Cards

Blackline Master 1.3

# 50 HANDS-ON ADVANCED Literacy Strategies

## 4 Decoding Bowling

**Figure 1.3**

### Skill

- ❏ Little lit learners: Onset and rime.
- ❏ Leveled-up lit learners: Digraphs.

### Materials per Small Group

- ❏ Toy bowling set or empty water bottles and ball
- ❏ Marker

# Part 1 Hands-On Word Recognition

## Directions

- ❏ Little lit learners: Choose one common CVC rime (i.e., *at, en, ig*) and write it on the ball. Brainstorm a list of CVC words that include the rime. Write the consonants for those words on the bowling pins (e.g., "at" pattern: write "r" or "c" on the pins to create the words *rat* or *cat*).
- ❏ Leveled-up lit learners: Choose one digraph (i.e., *sh, wh*) and write it on the ball. Brainstorm a list of words that include the digraph. For an additional challenge, include a mix of words that have a digraph at the beginning or end of the word. This will require students to determine if the digraph is added to the beginning or the end of the consonants to create a word. Write the consonants for those words on the bowling pins (e.g. if your digraph is *sh*, you could add *di* to a pin for students to create the word dish or *irt* for students to create the word shirt).

## Introduction

Begin this lesson by brainstorming words that include the same rime or digraph students will explore as they play decoding bowling. Share the letters and their sounds on the bowling pins and ball. Once the pins are knocked down, you will use the letters on the knocked down pins and bowling ball to create words. Model a game, thinking aloud together with students to create words using onset and rime [little lit] or digraphs [leveled-up lit].

## Hands-On Literacy Task

1. Students will work in groups of 2–4. One student will roll the ball, saying the rime [Little Lit] or digraph [leveled-up lit] sound.
2. Together they will use the ball and the pins to decode and create new words; then they will reset the bowling game.
3. Students will take turns rolling and continue reading words on the knocked down pins for the rest of the class.

## Whole Group or Small Group Reflection Prompt

"We played this game using the _____ pattern. If we use the pattern _____ next time, what are some of the words we can make?"

# 50 HANDS-ON ADVANCED Literacy Strategies

## 5 The Floor Is Lava

**Figure 1.4**

## Skill

- ❏ Little lit learners: Onset and rime.
- ❏ Leveled-up lit learners: Magic e/split digraph.

## Materials per Group

- ❏ 10 stepping stones cut from black paper
- ❏ White crayon – write the following on each stone:
    a. Little lit: Write the onset letters: *f, fr, h, l, b, bl, j, sm, d, cl*.
    b. Leveled-up lit: Write the words: *cub, kit, lit, hip, lip, bit, not, cut, tub, tap*.
- ❏ Letter stone with *og* [little lit learners] or *e* [leveled-up lit learners]

## Part 1 Hands-On Word Recognition

### Introduction

Place the stepping stones you created around the room in such a way that children can step, hop, skip, or jump from one stone to another. (Note: If you have a student in a wheelchair, please make sure to place the stones far enough apart that they can roll their chair easily from one stone to another.) This game is played just as it the regular floor is lava – by pretending the floor is lava – and students will move (step, hop, etc.) from one safe stepping stone to another. The twist is that students will hold the special stone that allows them to create a new word by putting the rime *og* for little lit learners or *e* for leveled-up lit learners. Model playing this game for the class. Invite a child to be your partner. Together you will take turns choosing which stone to move to. One partner will read the letter sounds or words on the stone. The second partner will put the stone on the ground next to the letters or word and together you will read the new word. (i.e., *fr-og* or bit- *bite*) Once you've created and read the new word, you can move on to the next word. If space is an issue, you can turn this into a table is lava game and have students "hop" from stone to stone using small dolls or action figures.

### Hands-On Literacy Task

1. Students will work in groups of 2 or 3.
2. Students will move from one stepping stone to the next taking turns reading the letter sounds or words on the stone. Next, they will place the *og* or *e* stone on their stepping stone to make a new word. Students will read the new word together.
3. The students will create as many words as possible by moving from word stone to the next stone during the time limit set by the teacher.

### Whole Group or Small Group Reflection Prompt

"How did the stepping stones change when you added the rime *og* [little lit] or magic *e* [leveled-up lit]?"

## 6 Seek and Find

### Skill

- ❏ Little lit learners: Segmenting syllables.
- ❏ Leveled-up lit learners: Segmenting phonemes.

# 50 HANDS-ON ADVANCED Literacy Strategies

Materials per Group

- ❏ Miscellaneous items children find around the classroom (see Figure 1.5).

## IDEAS FOR SYLLABLE SEEK AND FIND

pen
book
block
ball

paper
pencil
marker
journal

basketball
thesaurus
rectangle
computer

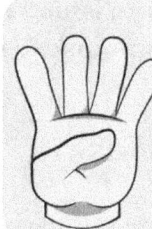
dictionary
calculator
aquarium
librarian

## IDEAS FOR PHONEME SEEK AND FIND

shoe
bow
boy
key

pen
book
face
glue

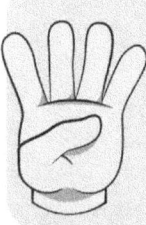
flag
lunch
block
globe

orange
street
plant
drink

**Figure 1.5**

## Introduction

In this exploration, little literacy learners will practice counting syllables, and leveled-up learners will count phonemes with a special seek and find game. Model the game for students. Begin by searching around the room for an item with the same number of syllables or phonemes. Think aloud as you clap or tap to segment the words: model examples and nonexamples. Little literacy learners will seek to find objects with 1, 2, 3, or 4 syllables. For the youngest little literacy number just beginning to explore syllables, begin by sorting objects as having 1 or 2 syllables. Leveled-up lit learners will seek and find objects with a specific number of phonemes. Focus on words with 2–5 sounds (i.e., 3 phonemes: pen, p-e-n).

## Hands-On Literacy Task

1. Begin by asking a child to randomly select a number from 1 to 4 [little lit] or 2 to 5 [leveled-up lit]. Have the students show the number on their fingers.
2. Students will *seek and find* around the room to find an object with the correct number of syllables or phonemes. If you are playing with the whole class, put children in pairs. Let one child search, and the other can be the accountability buddy checking the answer. (The children will reverse roles in step 4.)
3. Students share their object and count the syllables for the small group or accountability buddy. (If the object is large or high up, they can point it out.)
4. The other partner, or the next child, if working in small groups, will choose a number. Then they will repeat this game. Continue this pattern for as many rounds as possible in the permitted time.

## Whole Group or Small Group Reflection Prompt

"Think of an object we may see on the playground with more than ___ syllables or phonemes? Now think of a word with fewer syllables or phonemes."

# 7 Snowman Spy

## Skill

- ❏ Little lit learners: Isolating beginning sounds.
- ❏ Leveled-up lit learners: Isolating beginning, middle, or end sounds.

# 50 HANDS-ON ADVANCED Literacy Strategies

### Materials per Pair

- ❏ Snowman spy sensory bin or "snow globe"
    a. clear plastic bowl, jar to make a snow globe, or tub to make a sensory bin
    b. filler: biodegradable packing peanuts, cotton balls, or white kinetic sand
    c. laminated snowman spy pictures (color before laminating)
      * Use real objects as a scaffolded support, if necessary.
- ❏ Snowman challenge cards [little lit and leveled-up lit versions]

## Directions

Add filler and pictures or objects to a plastic bowl, jar, or tub.

## Introduction

Create your snow globe or snowman sensory bin using the directions above. Begin by modeling skills children will use for the I-Spy game today: beginning sounds [little lit] or identifying and matching words with the same beginning, middle, or ending sounds – including blends, digraphs, and diphthongs [leveled-up lit]. You can practice these skills by playing the game with one or two examples from the challenge card. Before you give a clue, chant: "I snowman spy with my little eye an object with the same ___ sound as ___." For children who need a more concrete experience, use small objects rather than pictures.

## Hands-On Literacy Task

1. Students will work in pairs to spy items from their snowman challenge cards. Students can take turns or work collaboratively.
2. After students complete the tasks on the snowman challenge card, invite them to do one of the following tasks:
    a. Play again. Find objects with different beginning (middle or ending) sounds.
    b. Take turns creating your own phonological clues to spy an object (i.e., "I snowman spy with my little eye an object with the same beginning sound as ice").

## Whole Group or Small Group Reflection Prompt

"We played our snowman spy game today by matching sounds that came at the beginning (middle or end) of the words on our snowman challenge cards. How might we use these snow globes or sensory bins) to practice rhyming?"

# SNOWMAN SPY OBJECTS

Color, laminate, cut apart and add to ispy snow globes!

I snowman spy with my little eye...

## Snowman Spy Pairs

| *Little Literacy Learners* | *Leveled-Up Literacy Learners* |
|---|---|
| piano, penguin | shell, shoe |
| candy cane, cup | snail, snowflake |
| dragon, drum | broom, spoon |
| wagon, wand | house, mouse |
| snail, snowflake | hand, wand |
| robot, reindeer | sock, block |

**Blackline Master 1.4**

© Allison Bemiss, *50 Hands-On Advanced Literacy Strategies for Young Learners, PreK–Grade 2*. Routledge 2023

# Snowman Challenge Card

Find an object in your snow globe with the **same** beginning sound as the picture's below.

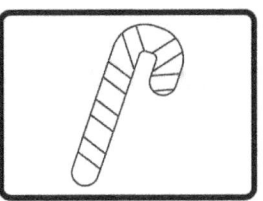

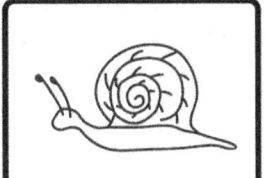

*Little Literacy Learners*

# Snowman Challenge Card

Find an object in your snow globe with the **same** beginning, middle, or ending sound as the picture's below.

beginning     middle     ending

*Leveled-Up Literacy Learners*

**Blackline Master 1.5**

# 50 HANDS-ON ADVANCED Literacy Strategies

# 8 Wizard Words

## Skill

- ❏ Little lit learners: Phoneme isolation: ending sounds.
- ❏ Leveled-up lit learners: Phoneme isolation: long vowel sounds.

## Materials per Group

- ❏ Wizard wand
- ❏ Wizard word cards
- ❏ Wizard word chart: pocket chart or hanging shoe organizer

## Introduction

Cut apart the wizard word cards and slip these words into the clear pockets of your wizard word chart. Tell students that your special wizard words rule for today: Little lit learners *words that end with the T sound*. Leveled-up lit learners *words with a long vowel sound*. Choose a word from your wizard word chart and model thinking aloud to determine if the word fits the wizard rule. (Be sure to model examples and nonexamples to match your wizard word rule.) When you find a word that matches your wizard rule, tap it with the wand, say the word, and whisper shout "Wizard Word," and take it out of the pocket chart. Model this a few times for the whole group. This game is versatile, and it can be used to sort any skill your students are currently exploring. If you are looking for an increased challenge in the leveled-up lit version, create wizard word cards with and without the *schwa* sound and allow students to do a *schwa* sort with this task.

## Hands-On Literacy Task

1. Students will work in groups of 2 to 4.
2. The child will find a wizard word that ends with the T sound [little lit] or long vowel sound [leveled-up lit], tap it with the wand, say the word, and whisper shout "Wizard Word," and take it out of the pocket chart.
3. Another child in the group will take the wand, and the activity starts over. Continue this pattern for as many rounds as you have time for during your lesson or until all the wizard words have been collected.

4. If students finish early, challenge the groups to choose two words and create a silly wizard sentence using two words.

## Whole Group or Small Group Reflection Prompt

"Take a look at the words you've pulled from your Wizard Words Chart. What patterns do you notice about your words?"

| feet | grape |
| bike | cat |
| wand | coat |
| boat | pumpkin |

**Blackline Master 1.6**

# 9 Silly Animal Sounds

## Skill

- ❏ Little lit learners: Deleting phonemes.
- ❏ Leveled-up lit learners: Deleting phonemes.

## Materials per Small Group

- ❏ 5–10 small animal figures or pictures (cow, dog, sheep, chicken, frog, goose)
- ❏ Paper bag
- ❏ Optional: animal movement cards

## Introduction

Little lit learners will explore deleting phonemes at the beginning of the word, while leveled-up literacy learners will vary the position of the deleted phoneme by choosing to delete the beginning, ending, or middle sound in the animal sound. Begin by showing children each animal in the bag and sharing the real sound it makes. Ask your students to close their eyes. Tell the students you will give them a clue to help them guess your mystery animal. Your clue will be the sound the animal makes, but with a silly twist. The animal noise will be missing the first sound! Pull an animal from the bag and share the sound the animal makes without the beginning sound. Remind the children to keep their eyes closed as you share the sound (e.g., cow: delete the *m* sound and say "oo"). Repeat the sound. Ask students to guess the animal and then tell you the missing sound (cow: "m" for "moo"). If you are playing with the gross motor twist, students will then make the silly animal sound (deleted phoneme sound) while they do the animal movement on the corresponding card for 30 seconds. Leveled-up lit learners can extend the challenge by varying the position of the deleted phoneme. Model the game again by deleting the ending sound or middle sound if there are more than two phonemes in the word. Then when children play the game below, they can choose to delete any phoneme in the animal sound.

## Hands-On Literacy Task

1. Students will work in groups of 2–4. One child will hold the bag, and the others will close their eyes as he pulls an animal from the bag. The child will share the "silly animal sound" with his classmates.

# 50 HANDS-ON ADVANCED Literacy Strategies

2    The other children will guess the animal based on the sound and share the missing sound. If you are playing the gross motor version, students will then move like that animal for 30 seconds together, making the silly animal sound.

3    The child with the bag will pass it to another student, and the game will continue.

## Whole Group or Small Group Reflection Prompt

"Think of two words that would sound the same if you deleted their beginning sounds."

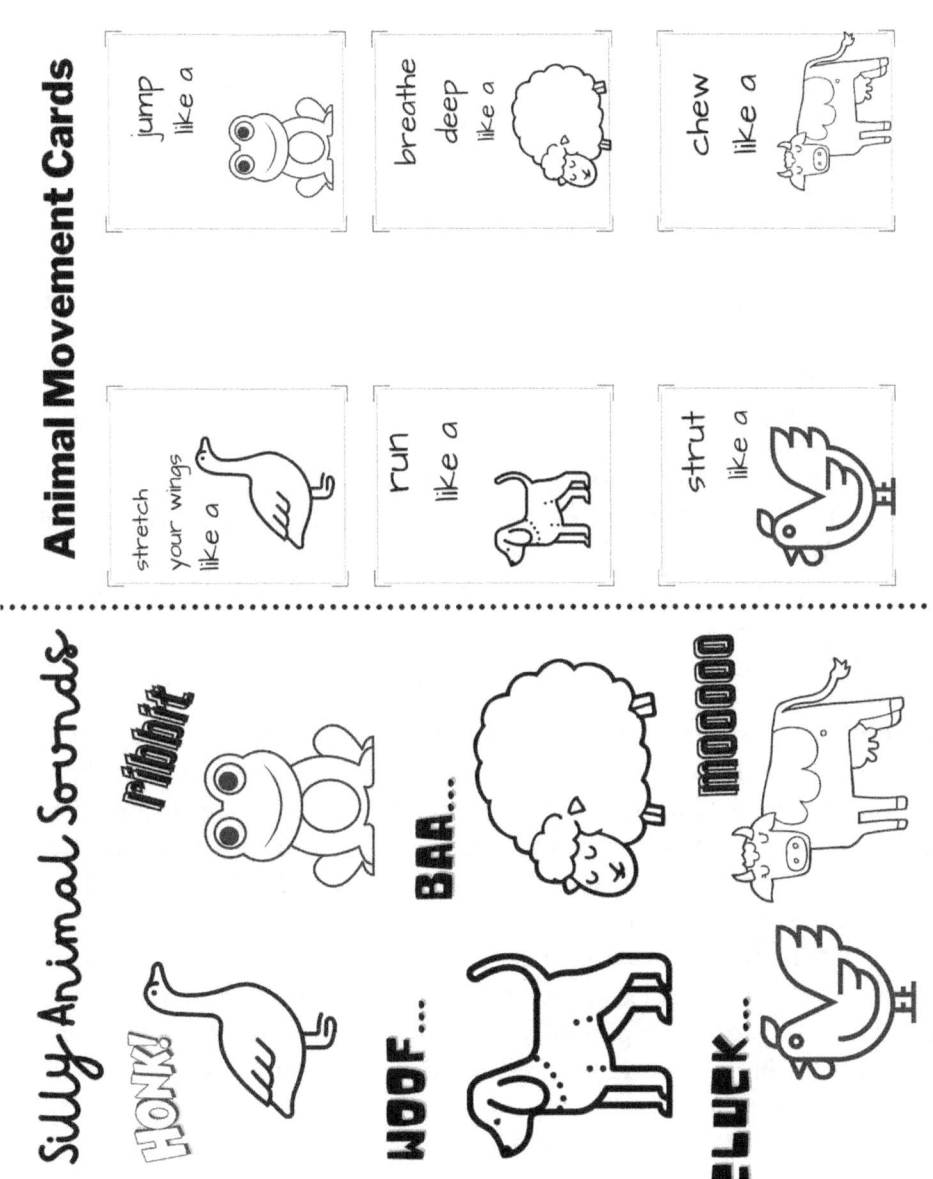

Blackline Master 1.7

# 10 Syllable Surgery

## Skill

- ❏ Little lit learners: Segmenting syllables or compound words.
- ❏ Leveled-up lit learners: Open/closed syllables.

## Materials per Small Group

- ❏ Surgery cards words or compound word pictures for the youngest little lit learners
- ❏ Scissors
- ❏ 1 sorting tray

   a. Little lit: Divide the tray into sections for 1 or 2 syllables.
   b. Leveled-up: Divide the tray into sections for open or closed syllable words.

## Introduction

Begin this lesson by reminding students that a vowel sound is cool because it's made without significant obstruction to airflow, meaning the air keeps flowing as the sound is made. This makes it a perfect letter to sing! Sing a vowel sound, then a consonant sound. (Try to sing a *b* as opposed to an *a*.) Let them hold their hands up to their mouth and feel the difference in the airflow. Review syllables and segment words into syllables.

Little lit learners will explore cutting the word cards into syllables and sorting by the number of syllables. If you are working with very young children, this task can be modified to be a phonological task by having the students segment, or cut, pictures of compound words into two parts to represent. Cards have been included for that version as well.

Leveled-up lit learners will divide a word into syllables and then sort it as an open or closed syllable. Model thinking aloud that an open syllable ends in a single vowel with a long sound (i.e., *no, a-corn*), while a closed syllable has a short vowel closed by a consonant (i.e., *not, picnic*)

*Not all of the word cards will be cut since some words only have one syllable. Explain that just like some people don't need surgery, not all of the word cards need surgery, and it's their job to determine if the cards need to be cut. Although they cannot all be cut, they can all be sorted.

### Hands-On Literacy Task

1. Students will work in small groups, perform surgery, cutting the words into syllables. Optional: Have the students hole punch and "stitch" the words back together with yarn.
2. Next, students will sort their words onto the correct tray. Children using compound word variation will not need to sort their words.

### Whole Group or Small Group Reflection Prompt

"How can dividing words into syllables or parts help us decode new words?"

# Syllable Surgery
## Compound Word Picture Cards

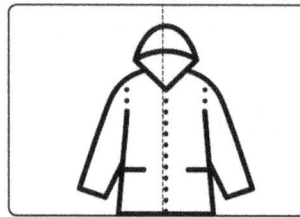 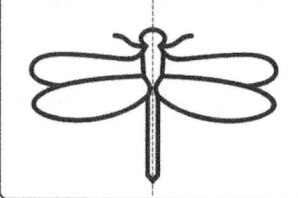 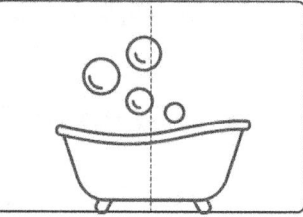

## Syllable Surgery Word Cards

| | |
|---|---|
| she | shell |
| he | hero |
| tiger | camp |
| picnic | baby |

**Blackline Master 1.8**

# 11 Backwards Day Hopscotch

## Skill

- ❏ Little lit learners: Reversing words (compound words).
- ❏ Leveled-up lit learners: Reversing phonemes.

## Materials per Small Group

- ❏ Backwards day hopscotch cards
- ❏ Bean bag or small stone
- ❏ Hopscotch board with backwards day hopscotch cards
    a. Outdoors: Create using sidewalk chalk.
    b. Indoors: Create on a white shower curtain or bulletin board paper.
- ❏ Word pairs:
    a. Little lit: sunflower:flower sun, cupcake:cake cup, football:ball foot, snowman:man snow, toothbrush:brush tooth, starfish:fish star, raincoat:coat rain, sunglasses:glasses sun
    b. Leveled-up: nap:pan, ten:net, gum:mug, sub:bus, top:pot, tug:gut, tea:eat.

## Directions

Cut apart and tape matching pairs to check answers. Place cards on squares.

## Introduction

It's backwards day! Students will be exploring reversing words in compound words [little literacy learners] or phoneme reversal [leveled-up literacy learners]. The small group will need enough room to spread out their hopscotch board. Practice phoneme reversal (rat:tar) or compound word reversal (rainbow:bow rain). Model the game. Toss a stone or bean bag onto one of the rectangles of the board and call out the word. Hop to the word. Little lit students will say the compound word in reversed order (i.e., sunglasses:glasses, sun). Leveled-up students will reverse the phonemes to say a new word (i.e., gum:m-u-g, mug). In both versions, students can flip the picture card over to check their answers. For a bit of gross motor fun, you can challenge the students to move backward across the hopscotch board.

# 50 HANDS-ON ADVANCED Literacy Strategies

### Hands-On Literacy Task

1. Students can play this in pairs or small groups.
2. One child will toss the bean bag onto one of the squares of the hopscotch board.
3. The child hops to the stone and calls out the reversal word or reversed compound word.
4. The child can check their answer by flipping up the card to check the back.
5. Continue this pattern with the next child in the group.

### Whole Group or Small Group Reflection Prompt

"Reversing sounds is a challenge, and everyone makes mistakes. What mistakes did you make today? Share your 'Oops, I learned . . .' moment from backwards day."

# Backwards Day Hopscotch

Little Lit Learners Version: Cut apart and tape matching sets front to back. Then place on hopscotch board.

Compound Words: starfish, toothbrush, snowman, sunflower

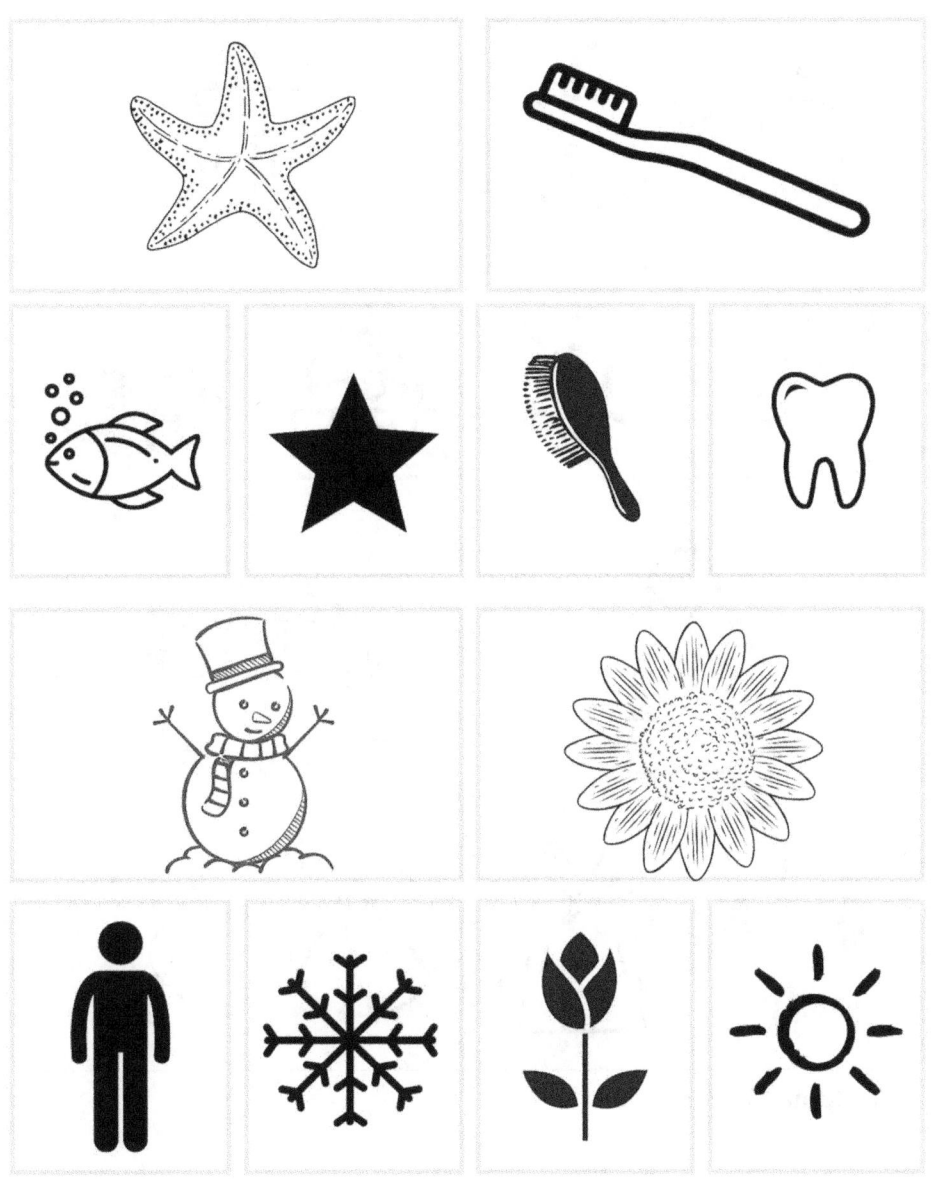

**Blackline Master 1.9**

© Allison Bemiss, *50 Hands-On Advanced Literacy Strategies for Young Learners, PreK-Grade 2*. Routledge 2023

# Backwards Day Hopscotch

Little Lit Learners Version: Cut apart and tape matching sets front to back. Then place on hopscotch board.

Compound Words: sunglasses, cupcake, raincoat, football

**Blackline Master 1.10**

© Allison Bemiss, *50 Hands-On Advanced Literacy Strategies for Young Learners, PreK-Grade 2*. Routledge 2023

# Backwards Day Hopscotch

Leveled-Up Lit Learners:
Cut apart and tape matching sets front to back.
Then place on hopscotch board.

## Word Pairs:
nap: pan, star: rats, ten: net,
top: pot, sub: bus, mug: gum

**Blackline Master 1.11**

# 50 HANDS-ON ADVANCED Literacy Strategies

## 12 Feed the Monster

**Figure 1.6**

### Skill

- ❏ Little lit learners: Phoneme isolation, sound-letter connection.
- ❏ Leveled-up lit learners: Phoneme reversal, sound-letter connection.

### Materials per Child

- ❏ Tissue box w/ monster printable taped on top
- ❏ Feed the monster cards [Little Lit and leveled-up lit learners]
  - \* Use real objects as scaffolded support, if necessary
  - \* Little lit learners adaptation: Objects with varied beginning sounds in lieu of cards.

# Part 1 Hands-On Word Recognition

## *Introduction*

Little lit learners will explore isolating phonemes at the beginning, middle, and end of a word by finding the common sound in a set of two pictures using their feed the monster cards. Students will then identify the corresponding letter and feed it to the monster. For the youngest little lit learners, use real objects for comparison to find the common sound in lieu of picture cards. In this version, the children will identify the beginning sound of the object and the corresponding letter. Students will feed that letter to the monster. Leveled-up lit learners will practice creating new words by reversing the phonemes of the word on the picture card. If you want your children to work strictly on phoneme reversal without seeing the letters of the written word you can adapt the card by covering up the word on the card prior to copying it for students.

For an additional challenge, ask students to notice if the vowel sound stays the same or changes.

## *Hands-On Literacy Task*

1. Students will work in small groups.
2. Little lit learners will take turns selecting a card, identifying the common phoneme and letter. Then feeding that letter to the monster. (See note above for adaptation for young students.) Leveled-up lit learners will select a card, reverse the word on the card to make a new word; next, they will build that word with their letters and feed those letters to the monster.
3. Students continue taking turns choosing feed the monster cards for their small group to explore together and then working through the same pattern listed above.

## *Whole Group or Small Group Reflection Prompt*

Little lit: "If the monster wants to eat the letter *b*, what are two objects he could have on his plate?"

Leveled-up lit: "Let's listen to the word rail and then the word liar, how do the vowel sounds differ? Why does the vowel sound change when we reverse the order?"

# FEED THE MONSTER:

Color, cut out, and glue on a tissue box.
(Don't forget to cut a hole for his mouth, he's hungry!)

**Blackline Master 1.12**

© Allison Bemiss, *50 Hands-On Advanced Literacy Strategies for Young Learners, PreK–Grade 2*. Routledge 2023

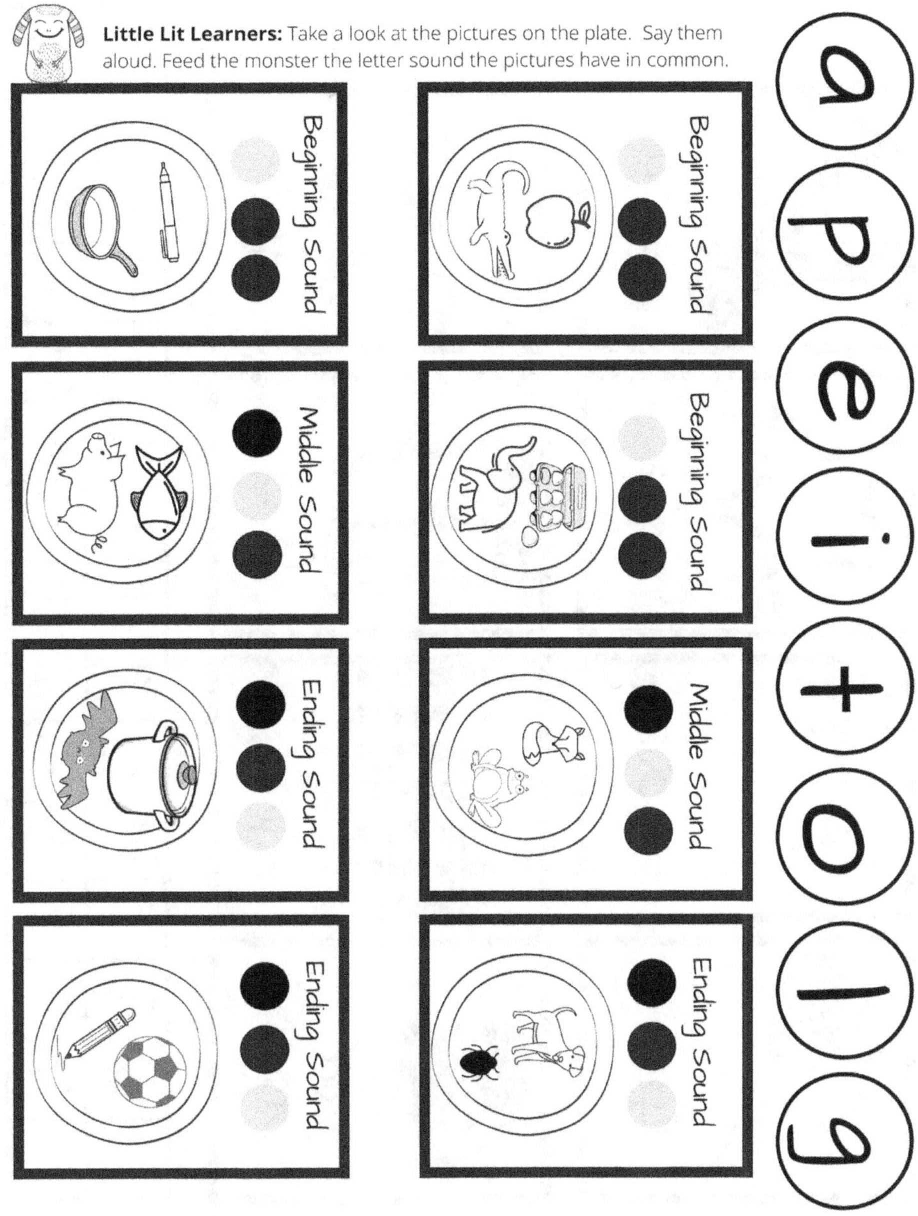

**Little Lit Learners:** Take a look at the pictures on the plate. Say them aloud. Feed the monster the letter sound the pictures have in common.

Blackline Master 1.13

© Allison Bemiss, *50 Hands-On Advanced Literacy Strategies for Young Learners, PreK-Grade 2*. Routledge 2023

**Blackline Master 1.14**

# Part 1 Hands-On Word Recognition

## 13 Buried Treasure

**Figure 1.7**

## Skill

- ❏ Little lit learners: *r* consonant blends.
- ❏ Leveled-up lit learners: *r* controlled vowel (*ar*, adaptable for other vowels + *r*).

## Materials per Group

- ❏ Plastic tub and sand
- ❏ Treasure picture cards*
    a. Little lit learners: crown, trash, grape, truck, frog, brush, dress, crab
    b. Leveled-up lit learners: star, jar, car, scarf, shark, target, card, arm
- ❏ Nonexample cards: rake, rabbit, railroad, cane, cat, rocket, fan, ribbon

   * Picture cards from the alternate version of the game can also be used as nonexample cards.

❏ Treasure chest (any empty box with treasure chest template pasted on the front)

    * If you have small objects or toys of these items, you can use those instead of pictures for an additional scaffold to support learners.

## Introduction

Welcome your students with your best pirate sounding "rrr" or "arrr!," explaining that today you will be helping the pirates search for their buried treasure. Each piece of treasure is a word with an "r" blend [little lit learners] or "ar" r controlled *a* sound [leveled-up learners]. Have your students repeat the word *cry* [lLittle lit] or *racecar* [leveled-up lit] as an example of these two patterns. Share that the buried treasure must have the *r* blend [little lit] or an r controlled vowel: *ar* [leveled-up lit] pattern. Any treasure they find will go on the treasure chest, while any other objects they find without the pattern are not treasure and should be left behind in the sand. Students can also keep a list of the treasure they find on a piece of paper or journal.

## Hands-On Literacy Task

1. Students will work in groups of 2 to 4.
2. Students will take turns finding an object/picture in the sand.
3. Then students will say the word together slowly a few times while listening to the sounds.
4. Last, they will sort the object/picture into the treasure chest if it has the *r* blend [little lit] or an r controlled vowel sound *ar* [leveled-up lit], and if it does not, leave it in the sand.

## Whole Group or Small Group Reflection Prompt

"What are two more words that could have been added as pirate treasure?"

## Little Literacy Learners: r blends

## Leveled-Up Literacy Learners: r controlled vowel (ar)

**Blackline Master 1.15**

## Non-Treasure Cards (Both Levels)

### Treasure Chest Template: Glue On Empty Box

**Blackline Master 1.16**

# 14 Wild Sounds Safari

## Skill

- ❏ Little lit learners: Consonant blends.
- ❏ Leveled-up lit learners: Consonant blends.

## Materials per Pair

- ❏ Safari card [little lit learners and leveled-up literacy learners)

## Introduction

Begin by introducing common blends students will use in today's task. Little lit version: initial consonant blends (*cl, gl, sl, dr, tr, ct*). Leveled-up version: final sound consonant blends (*st, nd, nk, rd, ck, nt*). As you introduce each one, practice finding something in the room with that sound. Encourage creativity in this safari as they track down words. Words can be an object (noun), something they see happening (verb), or a describing word (adjective or adverb). Write the word on a chart and underline the blend, you may also want to draw a corresponding picture. Model thinking aloud about each sound as you say the blend. For the youngest little lit learners, consider doing this task as a phonological awareness task (oral only) in a small group with the teacher, focusing on only one or two blends at a time, rather than introducing them all at once. (See Figure 1.8 for an example of words students may find at home or school.)

## Hands-On Literacy Task

1. Students will work in pairs.
2. The pair will work together on the wild sound safari searching for objects that have blends. Children who are writing independently can record the objects with blends they find in the appropriate box of the safari card.
3. The students will find as many words that match their blend safari card as possible during the time allotted for this activity.

# 50 HANDS-ON ADVANCED Literacy Strategies

## SCHOOL OR HOME SAFARI SAMPLE WORD LIST

Student's may not find words from every category. Encourage the kids to be creative. Verbs or describing words for objects they see can also be included.

| cl | sl | gl |
|---|---|---|
| closet | slide | glue |
| clock | sleep | glass |
| **dr** | **cr** | **tr** |
| drawing | cracker | tree |
| dress | crayon | trashcan |
| **-st** | **-rd** | **-ld** |
| first | bird | child |
| test | card | old |
| **-nt** | **-nd** | **-nk** |
| plant | land | sink |
| student | kind | drink |

**Figure 1.8**

## Whole Group or Small Group Reflection Prompt

"Read these blends aloud with your partner. Choose your favorite blend you found today. If you did this safari at home, which words might you have found?"

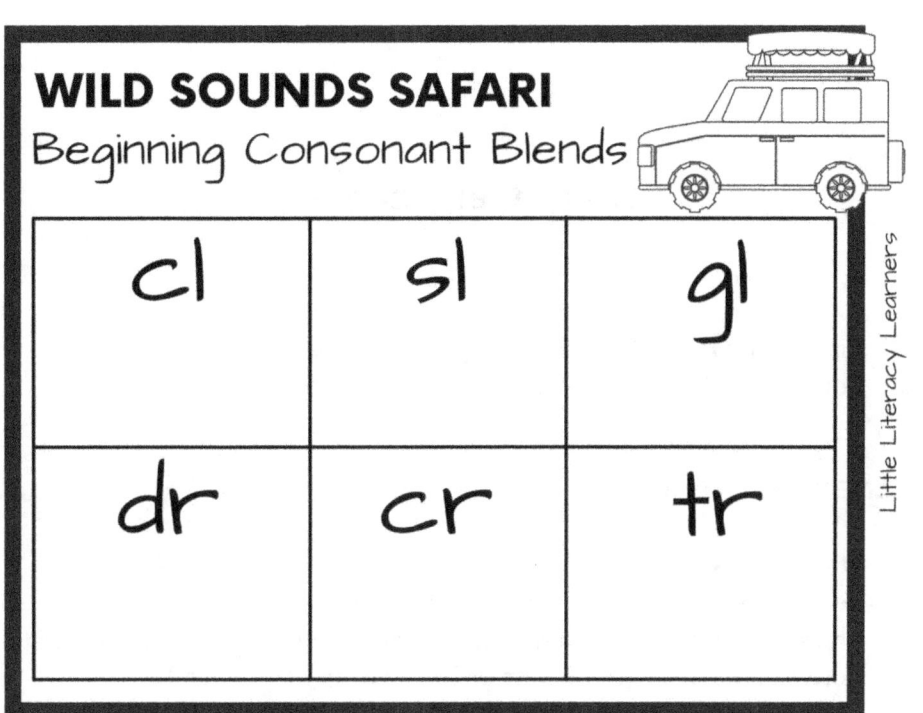

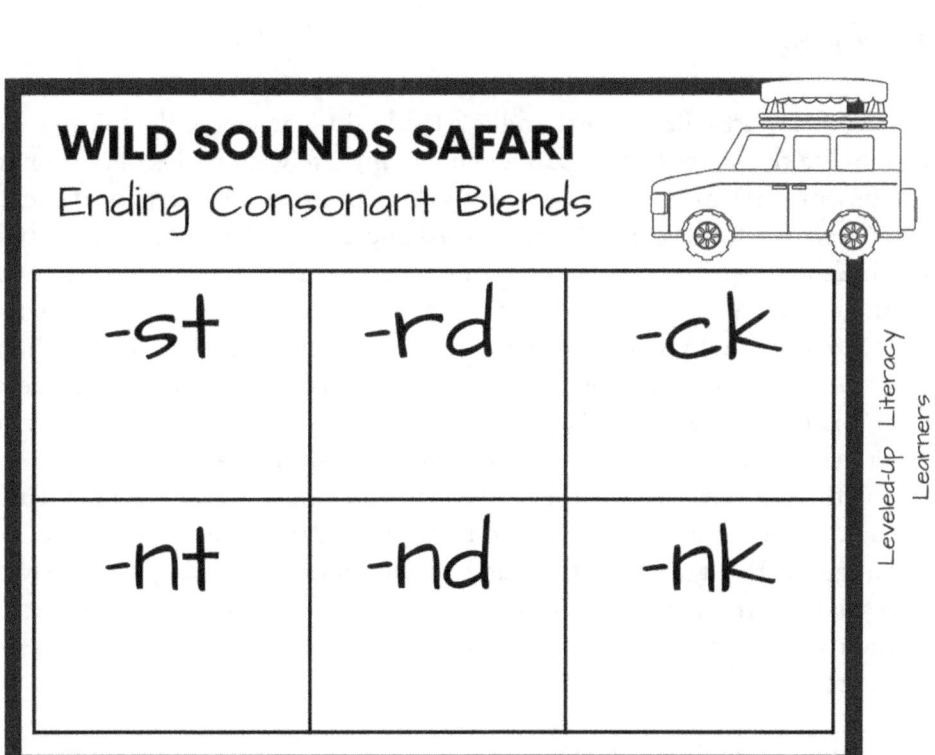

**Blackline Master 1.17**

© Allison Bemiss, *50 Hands-On Advanced Literacy Strategies for Young Learners, PreK–Grade 2*. Routledge 2023

# 50 HANDS-ON ADVANCED Literacy Strategies

## 15 Letter Teams

### Skill

- Little lit learners: Consonant digraphs (*sh*, *th*, *wh*, *ch*).
- Leveled-up lit learners: Vowel team (unpredictable pattern: *ea*).

### Materials per Pair

- Sticky notes
- Teamwork chart [little lit and leveled-up lit]
- Photos or small objects with *sh*, *th*, *wh*, *ch* sound [little lit learners]
- Letter cards or magnetic letters [leveled-up lit learners]

### Introduction

In this activity, little lit learners and leveled-up lit learners will explore letter teams. Begin this activity by sharing and writing a few examples of consonant digraphs [little lit learners] or vowel teams [leveled-up lit learners] on an anchor chart. Circle the letter teams in each word and explain that these two letters work together, just like your class works together. Tell the children that you need them to team up together to make words as a team (in pairs), using letter teams! Model the activity by putting a sticky note with one letter on your hand and the other letter on one of your student's hands. Hold your hands side by side to form the letter team (i.e., little lit learners *w-h*, leveled-up lit learners *e-a*). Use your hands with the sticky note letters and magnetic letters to create words with your pattern. For the leveled-up version, be sure to model words with each of the sounds the children will explore today (team, bread, steak). For the youngest little lit learners, this can be adapted to an oral language activity. Rather than having pairs of children build the words using magnetic letters. have them join hands to make the consonant digraph (i.e., *sh*), and they can sort objects on the letter team chart.

### Hands-On Literacy Task

1. Students will work in pairs.
2. Students will use their vowel team and the magnetic letters to create words with their letter team.

3 The students will write the words they create on their teamwork chart, sorting by sound.
4 The students will create as many words as possible during the time limit set by the teacher.

## Whole Group or Small Group Reflection Prompt

"What is another example of a letter team that works together in a word?"

**Blackline Master 1.18**

# TEAMWORK CHART
## Vowel Team: ea

**teach** | **bread** | **steak**

Words with the same vowel team sound as teach

Words with the same vowel team sound as bread

Words with the same vowel team sound as steak

**Blackline Master 1.19**

© Allison Bemiss, *50 Hands-On Advanced Literacy Strategies for Young Learners, PreK–Grade 2*. Routledge 2023

# 50 HANDS-ON ADVANCED Literacy Strategies

## 16 Mirror Mirror

### Skill

- ❏ Little lit learners: Blends.
- ❏ Leveled-up lit learners: Diphthongs.

### Materials per Pair

- ❏ Hand-held mirrors
- ❏ Sound spinner [little lit and leveled-up versions] (*see note for young learners).
- ❏ Fidget Spinner (draw an arrow on one arm of the spinner)

### Introduction

Begin this lesson by practicing the sounds of the blends [little lit learners] or diphthongs [leveled-up lit learners] on the sound spinner children will be using in the task. Work together to create a list of words with each of these letter patterns. You may want to write or draw them on an anchor chart so students can reference them later if they need to when they are generating words that match the letter pattern they spin. Play a model game with the students. As the spinner is spinning, have students say the rhyme: "Mirror, mirror in my hands, watch me make the sound where my spinner lands." Then students watch how their mouth and tongue move in the mirror as they say the sound and the word the fidget spinner is pointing to. Last, students will generate a word with the sound. (*For the youngest little lit learners, you can adapt this activity to be a letter/sound recognition task. Rather than using the sound spinner, put letters in a paper bag and have children pull a single letter from the bag to play the game.)

### Hands-On Literacy Task

1. Students will work in groups of 2 to 4. One student will spin the Fidget Spinner, saying the sounds of the blend [little lit] or diphthong [leveled-up lit] while they watch how their mouth moves in the mirror, noticing patterns.
2. Once they've identified and each practiced the sound, students will take turns generating a new word with that sound, watching their mouth move in the mirror as they say it.

3   The next student in the group will spin the sound spinner, and the game will continue.

## Whole Group or Small Group Reflection Prompt

"We watched our mouths move in the mirror as we said these sounds. What patterns did you notice? What sounds can you make with similar patterns? Which sounds can you make with different mouth movement patterns?"

# MIRROR MIRROR
## SOUND SPINNER: BLENDS
LITTLE LITERACY LEARNERS

| bl | cr | sk |
|---|---|---|
| sp | Draw an arrow on your fidget spinner and place it here. | fl |
| cl | sn | tr |

**Blackline Master 1.20**

**Blackline Master 1.21**

# 17 Building Words

## Skill

- ❏ Little lit learners: Substituting and blending words (compound words).
- ❏ Leveled-up lit learners: Substituting and blending phonemes.

## Materials per Small Group

- ❏ Blocks
- ❏ Counters

## Introduction

Students will create words by substituting words [little lit] or phonemes [leveled-up lit]. Students will use counters to represent each word in a compound word or phoneme in a word. Directions are listed below for little lit and leveled-up lit learners. Block towers: Both versions of this activity will use block towers to record the number of words they created in the activity. Students will put one block down for each new word.

## Hands-On Literacy Task

### Little Lit Learners

Play individually or in a small group with students. Begin with two counters, touching a counter for *rain* and a counter for *bow*, drag your finger across the counters as you blend to make the word *rainbow*. You will swap the counters for the corresponding word each time a swap is made (*see Figure 1.9*):

- ❏ rainbow (swap bow for coat) raincoat (swap coat for drop) raindrop = 3 block tower
- ❏ sunshine (swap shine for glasses) sunglasses (swap sun for eye) eyeglasses (swap glasses for ball) eyeball (swap eye for base) baseball = 4 block tower

Challenge: Create the tallest tower beginning with the word *toothpaste*.

Part 1 Hands-On Word Recognition

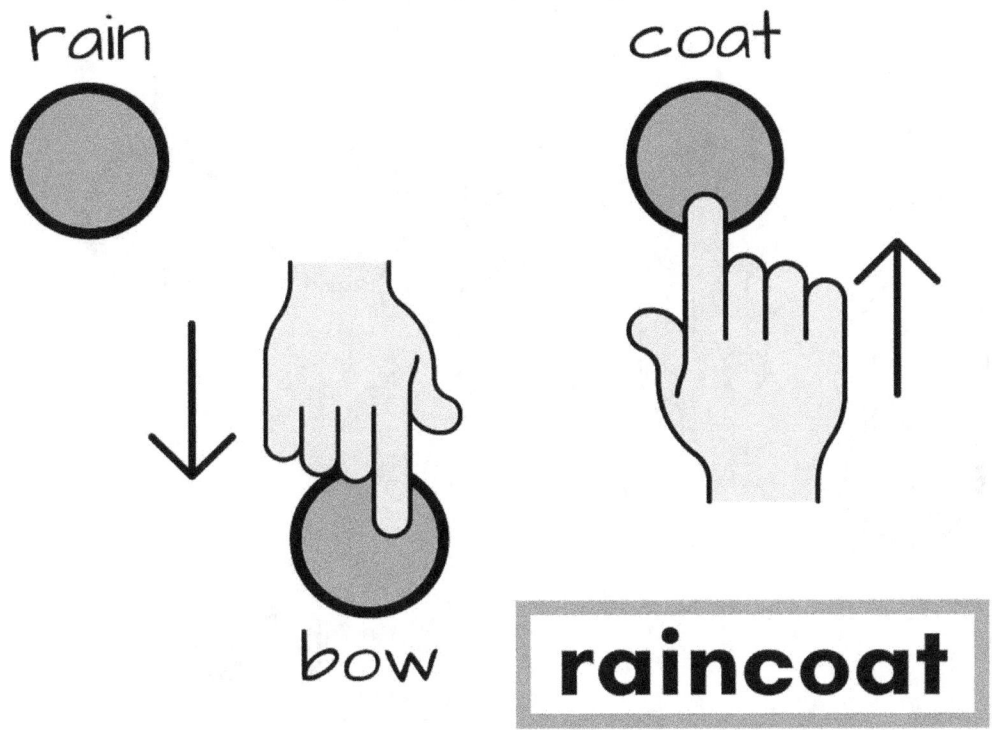

**Figure 1.9**

### Leveled-Up Lit Learners

Use letter sounds as you give directions. Each sound in the word is represented by one counter (i.e., *c-a-t* is 3 counters; *f-l-a-t* is 4 counters). (See Figure 1.10.)

Model: cat (swap *c* for *fl*) flat (swap *t* for *g*) flag (swap *fl* for *b*) bag = 4 block tower.

1. Students can play in pairs or small groups. All groups will start with the word "dog."

# 50 HANDS-ON ADVANCED Literacy Strategies

# Leveled-Up Lit Learners

cat to flat

swap **c** for **fl**

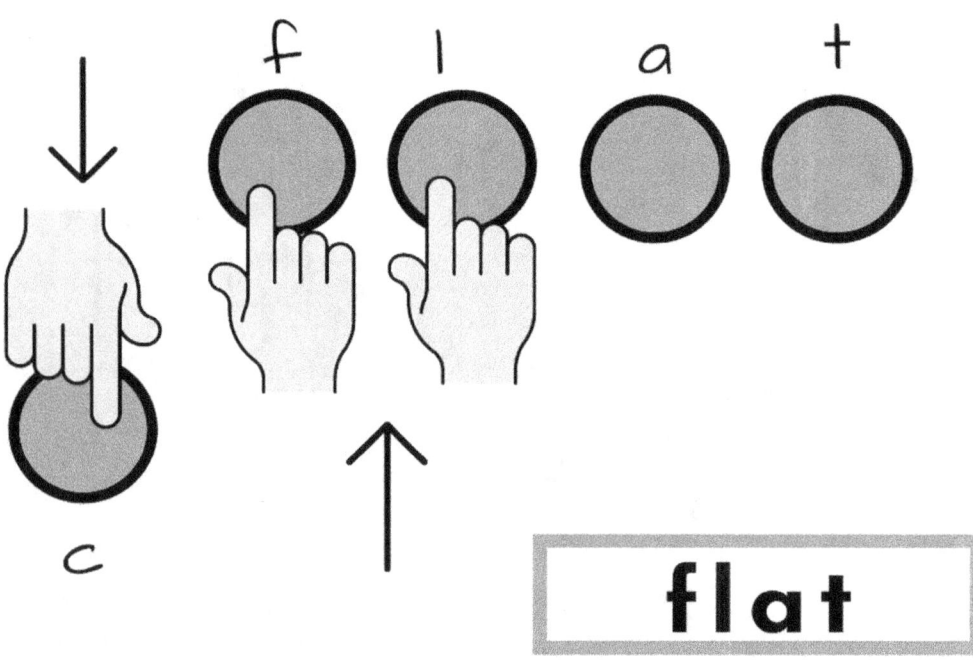

**Figure 1.10**

2. Students take turns brainstorming sound swaps to create new words using counters. Each time a new word is created the group adds another block to their tower.
3. Give a few minutes per word. Play as many rounds as time allows.

## Whole Group or Small Group Reflection Prompt

"Swapping sounds can help us read and say new words. How do you think practicing swapping sounds can help us build new words as we are writing?"

# 18 Fairy Tale Forest Map

## Skill

- ❏ Little lit learners: Substituting phonemes (CVC only).
- ❏ Leveled-up lit learners: Substituting phonemes.

## Materials per Small Group

- ❏ Letters cards or magnetic letters
- ❏ Fairytale forest map game board
- ❏ Small object for game piece (i.e., trinket, toy, rock, craft puff)

## Game Board Prep Directions

Choose a word chain from the charts in Figures 1.11 and 1.12 or create your own. Add one direction to each box of the game board. See Figure 1.13 for an example.

## Introduction

This task is similar to "building words" in that little literacy learners and leveled-up lit learners will create words by substituting phonemes. The youngest learners will use CVC pattern words, while children at a higher level of readiness will substitute words with blends, digraphs, and trigraphs. This lesson bridges from a strictly phonological activity into phonics by adding the use of letters in lieu of counters. Begin this activity by practicing a few phonological swaps using magnetic letters (i.e., little lit: cat: swap *t* for *p*, cap: swap *a* for *u*, cup. Leveled-up: skill: swap *sk* for *st*, still: swap *ll* for *tch*, stitch). Rather than using counters to keep track of sound swaps like they did in the task, "Building Words," students will be moving the letters as they make swaps to create new words.

## Hands-On Literacy Task

1. Students should work in small groups with the teacher until they are familiar enough with the concept to work individually or in pairs.
2. Students will build the starting word with their letters and place their game piece on the starting box of the game board.

# 50 HANDS-ON ADVANCED Literacy Strategies

## Little Lit Learners
### Substutiting Phonemes (CVC)

dog
swap the d for l
swap the o for e
swap the l for p
swap the g for t
swap the p for s
swap the e for i
Name your word.

---

rat
swap the r for s
swap the s for b
swap the a for i
swap the b for l
swap the t for p
swap the l for d
Name your word.

### Fairytale Forest Game Directions

Figure 1.11

## Leveled-Up Lit Learners Substuting Phonemes

cash
swap the c for d
swap the a for i
swap the d for w
swap the sh for n
swap the w for sh
swap the sh for ch
Name your word.

---

watch
swap the w for scr
swap the tch for p
swap the scr for cl
swap the a for i
swap the cl for sh
swap the p for rt
Name your word.

## Fairytale Forest Game Directions

**Figure 1.12**

# 50 HANDS-ON ADVANCED Literacy Strategies

Figure 1.13

3. Students take turns creating new words following the directions on their game board.
4. Students will continue playing until they finish the map.
5. For an additional challenge, give students a blank game board and have them design their own game board with letter swap directions.

### Whole Group or Small Group Reflection Prompt

"Swapping sounds can help us read and say new words. Work with a partner to brainstorm a word of your choice. Now, make a letter swap to make a new word!"

# Fairy Tale Forest Map

**Blackline Master 1.22**

## 19 Say It, Create It

### Skill

❏ Little lit learners: Phoneme-grapheme mapping or orthographic mapping.
❏ Leveled-up lit learners: Phoneme-grapheme mapping or orthographic mapping.

### Materials per Child

❏ Say it, create it! laminated workmat
❏ Wikki Stix™, pipe cleaners, playdough, or other hands-on material of choice
❏ Counters
❏ Craft sticks: write words at the appropriate level of challenge for your students
❏ Dry erase markers

### Introduction

Begin by preparing a set of craft sticks with words to match the readiness levels or needs of the small group of students you are working with for this task. In this exploration, little lit learners and leveled-up lit learners will explore phoneme grapheme mapping also known as orthographic mapping. Do this activity in a small group with a teacher. Show children the say it, create it workmat. Model each task on the mat. Ask a child to select a craft stick. You will read the word aloud to the students. Have students close their eyes and visualize the word meaning (i.e., for the word *said*, visualize two people talking.) Invite them to share what they see with a friend. Students will repeat the word after you 3 times, high fiving a friend each time they say it. Ask students to high five a friend as they say the word, then practice saying each sound of the word together. Next students map the word by putting down counters to represent each sound and write the corresponding letter(s) in the sound boxes. A note about irregular words: when mapping an irregular word pattern, point the irregular sound and spelling out to students. Then note it in some way on their map. Many teachers have students draw a heart over these irregular patterns to note that these patterns must be learned by heart (Farrell, Hunter, and Osenga, 2020). Last, students will create their word on the workmat using the hands-on material provided.

# 50 HANDS-ON ADVANCED Literacy Strategies

## Hands-On Literacy Task

1. Students will work in small group, selecting a craft stick to explore together. Then repeating the word after the teacher, visualizing the word, high fiving a friend each time they repeat the word, mapping the word, and doing the *create it* portion independently.
2. Students continue exploring with this pattern for the remainder of the small group time.

## Whole Group or Small Group Reflection Prompt

"Choose one word that you created today and practice spelling it and using it in a sentence."

# Say it, Create it!

 Say it!

High five it!

 See it!

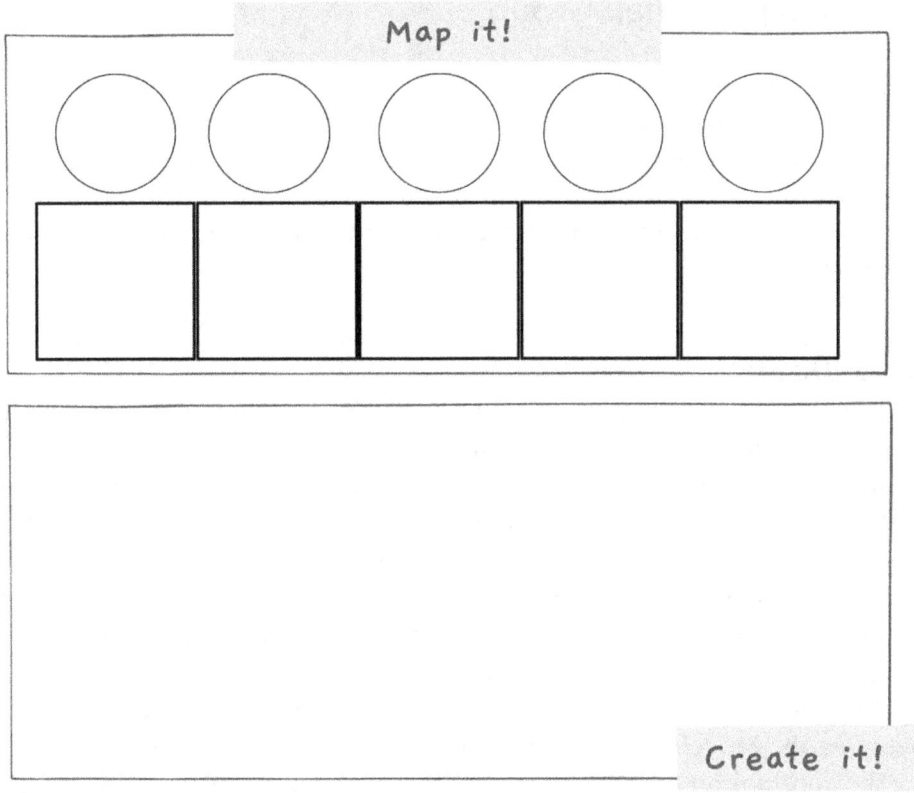

Map it!

Create it!

**Blackline Master 1.23**

# 20 Dramatic Dominos

## Skill

- ❏ Little lit learners: Fluency: oral language only.
- ❏ Leveled-up lit learners: Fluency.

## Materials per Small Group

- ❏ Nursery rhyme cards
- ❏ Blank dominos or blocks
- ❏ Dramatic domino printables (nursery rhyme and fluency prompts)

Glue a nursery rhyme printable to one side of the domino and fluency printable to the other.

## Introduction

In this exploration, students will explore fluency using nursery rhymes. Little lit learners will play dramatic dominos using nursery rhymes or familiar songs. (If they do not yet know these nursery rhymes, take some time to enjoy the songs with them throughout your day.) You may also want to share the nursery rhyme cards with families as a family literacy activity to enjoy at home. Once they know a few of the nursery rhymes, add those labels to the dominos and play this game together as an oral language task. Leveled-up lit learners will practice reciting or reading nursery rhymes using the dominos and nursery rhyme cards. Model playing the dramatic domino game with your students. Lay the dominos on the table, picture side up. Choose one at random to begin. Recite the nursery rhyme to match the domino's instructions with the fluency direction (i.e., spider and robot domino: read/recite "Itsy Bitsy Spider" in the voice of a robot.)

## Hands-On Literacy Task

1. Students will work in groups of 2 to 4. All dominos should be turned with the directions facing up.
2. The first student will choose one domino. The child will read or recite the nursery rhyme using the fluency direction on the dramatic domino then lay it down to start the game.

3. The second student will choose a domino with the same picture for the nursery rhyme or fluency prompt and line it up, matching the domino already out on the board. They will read/recite the nursery rhyme matching the directions on the domino they put down.
4. Students will continue playing this game with this pattern.

## Whole Group or Small Group Reflection Prompt

"I wonder how reciting or reading nursery rhymes in fun voices can help us be better readers."

# Dramatic Domino Pictures

Directions: Place one nursery rhyme and one fluency picture on each domino.

Sample:

 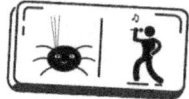  

## Nursery Rhyme

## Fluency
(Read like a...)

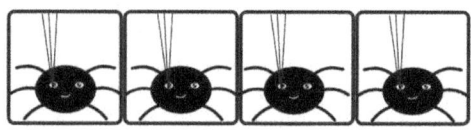    

**Blackline Master 1.24**

© Allison Bemiss, *50 Hands-On Advanced Literacy Strategies for Young Learners, PreK–Grade 2*. Routledge 2023

# Nursery Rhyme Cards

## Jack and Jill

Jack and Jill went up the hill
To fetch a pail of water;
Jack fell down and broke his crown,
And Jill came tumbling after.

## Itsy Bitsy Spider

The itsy bitsy spider
went up the water spout.
Down came the rain, and
washed the spider out.
Out came the sun, and
dried up all the rain,
and the itsy bitsy spider
went up the spout again.

Humpty Dumpty
sat on a wall
Humpty Dumpty
had a great fall
All the king's horses
and all the king's men
Couldn't put Humpty together again

## Humpty Dumpty

## This Little Piggy

 This little piggy went to market,

 This little piggy stayed home,

 This little piggy had roast beef,

 This little piggy had none.

 This little piggy went ...

Wee, wee, wee,
all the way home!

**Blackline Master 1.25**

© Allison Bemiss, *50 Hands-On Advanced Literacy Strategies for Young Learners, PreK-Grade 2*. Routledge 2023

## References

Farrell, L., Hunter, M., and Osenga, T. (2020, November 11). *A new model for teaching high-frequency words.* Reading Rockets. https://www.readingrockets.org/article/new-model-teaching-high-frequency-words

Gough, P. and Tunmer, W. (1986). Decoding, reading, and reading disability. *Remedial and Special Education, 7,* 6–10.

Strouse, G. A., Nyhout, A., and Ganea, P. A. (2018). The role of book features in young children's transfer of information from picture books to real-world contexts. *Frontiers in Psychology, 9,* 50.

# PART 2

# Hands-On Language Comprehension

In the Reading Rope shared in the Introduction of this book background knowledge, vocabulary, language structure, verbal reasoning, and literacy knowledge are listed as the threads of language comprehension. The hands-on, minds-on experiences shared in this section focus on skills within these categories, including oral language comprehension – semantics, syntax, morphemes, and pragmatics; vocabulary – exploring tiers, homophones, idioms, synonyms, and antonyms; critical reasoning and creative thinking strategies – making inferences, connecting to schema, visualizing, story analysis, and questioning; literacy knowledge – nonfiction text features and fictional story elements.

    The *little literacy learners* version of these tasks will primarily focus on the oral language components of each of these skills, suggesting picture or scaffolded support for the youngest children who are not yet readers. The *leveled-up literacy learners* version will sometimes include written reflection or more choices for the children to ponder as they explore.

    If students are just beginning to explore a skill, regardless of age or level, these tasks should be done in small groups with an adult. It is imperative that young students explore in an environment with modeling and rich language use. One great way to establish that support is to work in small groups alongside your students. However, if these tasks provide an additional layer of support or extension opportunity for a previously taught skill, students may be able to complete these tasks in a small group with only other children

DOI: 10.4324/9781003306627-3

(Mashburn, Justice, Downer, and Pianta, 2009). If students are working in a small group without an adult, it is important that there is an adult who models the task at the beginning of the work time and then periodically floats from group to group checking in to assess for students' understanding and that they are working at the appropriate level of challenge. As with the previous section of tasks, these small group tasks can be completed in a short period of time (typically 15–30 minutes), and many would work well as a part of a literacy center rotation.

Ragamuffin, far out, cool, bee's knees, no cap, that's fine – language, both written and spoken, is ever changing. As the parent of a teen, I'm learning every day that words (or emojis) I thought meant one thing now mean another. And it's not just slang; new words are added to the dictionary every year. The Covid-19 pandemic brought a whole new list of words into our world, including super-spreader, vaccine passport, and digital nomad. Sometimes as literacy teachers, we think we are teaching children to understand the printed and spoken language that already exists, and we are. However, it is equally important that we give our students the tools to figure out the language patterns and words that don't exist yet but will come to exist in their lifetime. Literacy instruction is a science; therefore, like all other sciences, it will be ever changing (Shanahan and Lonigan, 2013).

Giving students time to explore and develop strategies that help provide a deeper understanding of language (both written and spoken) is an imperative step in building a young learner's foundation for literacy and critical thinking. The language comprehension experiences in this book are meant to be engaging, multisensory, universally designed, hands-on, and minds-on opportunities to strengthen a wide variety of comprehension skills.

## 21 Ca-TOWER-Gories: Building Vocabulary

### Skill

- ❏ Little lit learners: Vocabulary: categories.
- ❏ Leveled-up lit learners: Vocabulary: categories.

### Materials per Group

- ❏ Wooden blocks
- ❏ Blank note cards to create "ca-tower-gorie" cards

Part 2 Hands-On Language Comprehension

**Figure 2.1**

# 50 HANDS-ON ADVANCED Literacy Strategies

### Directions

Create a list of 5 to 10 category vocabulary words you'd like your students to explore and write each one on a notecard. Or better yet, let your students help you collect words over time. For younger learners, common nouns or verbs work well (i.e., eat, school, or play). For older students, look for words in the books or content they are currently reading.

### Introduction

Tell the children today they will explore words! Introduce the word *category* to your students. A silverware tray with various types or sizes of spoon and fork is a good visual. You can show children that although the spoons may be made of different materials, colors, or sizes, they can get sorted together in the silverware tray. Sharing with them that today you will practice sharing words that would all fit in the same category. Get out your blocks and model an example with your students, inviting them to play along with you. Little lit learners will use a familiar word (i.e., *eat*: chew, swallow, consume, bite, taste, pig out). Leveled-up lit learners can use a word from a content you are studying (i.e., *animal*: bear or specific example, vertebrate, creature). Each time you say a word, add a block to your tower. As an option, students can record their words on paper or you can create a chart to capture their words. Groups will continue building towers until the tower tumbles. At that point, they will choose a new word.

### Hands-On Literacy Task

1. A child will choose the first category word card, share a word that fits within that category, and lay the first block of the tower. Then students will take turns adding a block as they each share a new word fitting within that category.
2. When the tower tumbles, it's time to choose a new category word and build a new tower.
3. Optional: students can record their words on a sheet of paper.

### Whole Group or Small Group Reflection Prompt

"Think of at least one word one of your teammates shared that you found interesting. What made the word interesting – was it new, unexpected, silly . . . ?"

# 22 Jack In the Box

## Skill

- ❏ Little lit learners: Vocabulary/inference.
- ❏ Leveled-up lit learners: Vocabulary/inference.

## Materials per Group

- ❏ Jack in the Box toy
- ❏ Blank note cards to create vocabulary cards

## Directions

Choose 5 to 10 words you would like your children to explore. It can be content area words, high frequency words, or any word of your choice. Then you will use the blank note cards to make a card for each word. Little lit learners cards can be created using pictures or environmental print. Leveled-up lit learners can use text only, and you may consider using content area words matching their units of study.

## Introduction

Little lit learners and leveled-up lit learners will explore generating and listening to clues and making inferences to guess a vocabulary word in this activity. Begin by teaching children the traditional Jack in the Box nursery rhyme to introduce the toy to those who may not have seen one before. "Jack-in-the-box, you sit so still [fist your hand with the thumb inside]. Won't you come out? [pop out your thumb] Yes, I will!" Model a game for the students. Invite a few children to play with you. Turn the cards upside down. You will be the first clue giver, flip a card over, and look at the word without showing it to your group. Give 1 clue to help your team guess the word. Then let one group member guess the word and crank the Jack in the Box one time. If the guess was not correct, give another clue and let another group member crank the Jack in the Box. The goal is for the group to guess the word before Jack pops out!

## Hands-On Literacy Task

1. The group will select one child to be the first "clue giver." That child will choose the first word card and give a clue. Each child will guess the

# 50 HANDS-ON ADVANCED Literacy Strategies

word and crank the Jack in the Box one time. If the guess was not correct, the clue giver shares another clue and lets another group member crank the Jack in the Box. Guess the word before Jack pops out!

2. After the word is guessed or Jack pops out, the next child will take the role of the clue giver, and the game will continue with a new vocabulary word. If Jack pops out before the word is guessed, the clue giver will share the vocabulary word.

## Whole Group or Small Group Reflection Prompt

"Choose 1 word today and think of a word that means almost the same as that word."

## 23 Word Mural

Figure 2.2

## Skill

- ❏ Little lit learners: Semantics/visualizing.
- ❏ Leveled-up lit learners: Semantics/visualizing.

## Materials per Class

- ❏ Newsprint roll or bulletin board paper

## Introduction

Give students a few days or weeks to collect words they find interesting. Students can find words they hear throughout the day, or it can be words encountered during reading instruction as you explore text or media together. Select a word for the class to explore and write it really large on a sheet of newsprint or bulletin board paper. This will serve as your final mural. If you are working with very young students, you may want to include a picture, but this is optional, as they will be providing artwork to accompany the word as a part of the project. Put students in small groups of 2 to 4. Cut the paper into as many pieces as you need to give a portion of the mural to each group.

Little lit learners and leveled-up lit learners will explore semantics and visualizing vocabulary. The differentiation will occur with the words you choose and the ideas you give them for things they can include on their portion of the mural. For example, you may choose to have the youngest learners draw pictures to represent the word and include letter strings of words related to the mural word. Consider using sign language to introduce the word as an additional extension for young children. Increase the challenge by not only asking children to draw pictures and create definitions or sentences, but also inviting them to do tasks with the mural word matching skills you've studied like generating synonyms or antonyms, creating semantic maps, or writing word sums (see "Morphology Tree"). Match your guidelines for the small groups' mural piece to the developmental readiness level and skills of students.

## Hands-On Literacy Task

1. The teacher or class will select the word in advance and write it on a large piece of paper. The paper will be cut into several pieces. Students

will work in groups of 2 to 4. Each group will receive a piece of the mural and will be responsible for drawing and writing on that piece of paper to represent the meaning of the mural word.
2   The teacher or groups will then tape their pieces together to create the mural.

## Whole Group or Small Group Reflection Prompt

"How are each group's mural pieces similar? How are they different?"

# 24 Homophone Hockey

## Skill

- ❏ Little lit learners: Homophones.
- ❏ Leveled-up lit learners: Homophones.

## Materials per Group

- ❏ 6 to 12 homophone (plastic) eggs (see Figure 2.3 for homophone word list)
- ❏ Little lit: prepare plastic eggs with a matching homophone pair on each side
- ❏ Leveled-up lit: prepare with homophone and definition on each side
- ❏ Box or basket tipped on the side (goal)
- ❏ Broom (hockey stick) *Use a craft stick if you are creating a tabletop version of the game.

## Introduction

Choose 6 to 12 homophone pairs for your children to practice. Then use the directions in the materials section to prepare your plastic eggs for the game. You may want to let your children help label each side of the plastic egg for their game.

Little lit learners will be matching pairs of homophones on the plastic eggs and then shooting them in their goals. If you are working with little learners who are not yet readers, use pictures on the plastic eggs alongside the words.

# HOMOPHONE HOCKEY WORD LISTS

| Little Literacy Learners | Leveled-Up Literacy Learners |
|---|---|
| sea/see<br>I/eye<br>for/four<br>eight/ate<br>meat/meet<br>sun/son<br>tale/tail<br>toe/tow<br>blue/blew<br>won/one | two/to/too<br>their/they're/there<br>aloud/allowed<br>hole/whole<br>knight/night<br>right/write<br>maid/made<br>vain/vein<br>thrown/throne |

**Figure 2.3**

Leveled-up lit learners will be matching definitions to the homophone first and then grouping homophones together. Once they have matched the word to the definition, and then grouped the pair (or triad) of homophones together, they will shoot their plastic eggs into the goal. Model a game first for your students as a mini lesson. Students can take turns shooting their homophone hockey eggs into the goal.

*Modify this to be a tabletop version by using craft sticks and a small basket or box as the goal.

## Hands-On Literacy Task

1. Open the plastic eggs and scatter them around the area. Students will work together to find the matching homophones for a plastic egg [little lit] or the homophone to its definition and then group the pair or triad of homophone eggs together [leveled-up].

# 50 HANDS-ON ADVANCED Literacy Strategies

2  The children will then take turns shooting their homophone egg(s) into the goal. Continue playing the game until all of the eggs have been shot on goal.

## Whole Group or Small Group Reflection Prompt

"Homophone humor challenge: Choose one set of homophones you played hockey with today. Think of a silly sentence that uses both words."

# 25 Synonym Splash

## Skill

- ❏ Little lit learners: Synonyms.
- ❏ Leveled-up lit learners: Synonyms.

## Materials per Group

- ❏ Bowl of water (waterless version: use a piece of blue paper)
- ❏ 10 synonym rubber duckies* (See Figure 2.4 for synonym word lists.)
    a. Little lit: Choose 5 pairs of synonym words and write each word on the bottom of a duck.
    b. Leveled-up lit: Choose 10 words you would like for students to use to generate synonyms and write one word on the bottom of each duck.

## Introduction

Little lit learners will be matching pairs of synonyms on the ducks in the duck pond. If you are working with little learners who are not yet readers, use pictures on the rubber duckies alongside the words. If you are adding pictures for your young learners on the bottom of a duck that will go on the water, cover it in clear packing tape or contact paper to make it waterproof.

Leveled-up lit learners will be selecting a duck, and then each group member will take turns generating and sharing synonym word(s) with their small group. Begin this activity by modeling a game first for your students as a mini lesson. Students can take turns selecting a duck from the pond and matching synonyms [little lit] or generating synonyms [leveled-up].

# SYNONYM SPLASH WORD LISTS

| Little Literacy Learners<br><br>Synonym Pairs | Leveled-Up Literacy Learners<br><br>Words to Generate Synonyms |
|---|---|
| big/large<br>happy/glad<br>laugh/giggle<br>little/tiny<br>scream/yell<br>difficult/challenge<br>child/kid<br>quiet/silent<br>garbage/trash<br>gift/present | gather<br>difficult<br>enjoy<br>quick<br>unlucky<br>simple<br>excellent<br>delicious<br>error<br>beautiful<br>quiet |

**Figure 2.4**

# 50 HANDS-ON ADVANCED Literacy Strategies

*You can modify this to be a waterless version by having the ducks on a pretend paper pond rather than a bowl of water. The game is also easily adaptable to practice antonyms.

### Hands-On Literacy Task

1  The students will play this game in groups of 2 to 4. Students will work together to find the matching synonyms for each rubber ducky [little lit], or they will randomly select a duck from the pond and take turns generating synonyms for each word [leveled-up].
2  The children will then take turns selecting a rubber ducky and matching [little lit] or generating [leveled-up] synonyms. Continue playing the game until all of the ducks have been used or as long as time permits.

### Whole Group or Small Group Reflection Prompt

"Choose one rubber duck from the pond. Share the synonym for that duck. Say or write a sentence with the word on the duck, then say the same sentence with a synonym. Which word works best in the sentence?"

## 26 ANTonyms In the Pants

### Skill

- ❏ Little lit learners: Antonyms.
- ❏ Leveled-up lit learners: Antonyms.

### Materials per Group

- ❏ Ants in the Pants™ game
- ❏ 10 copies of the antonym ant cards* (See Figure 2.5 for word lists.)
    a. Little lit: Choose 4 pairs of antonyms.
    b. Leveled-up lit: Choose 8 antonyms.

### Introduction

Little lit learners will match pairs of antonyms on the ant cards. If you are working with young children who are not yet readers, add pictures on the ant cards

# ANTONYMS IN THE PANTS WORD LISTS

| Little Literacy Learners<br>Antonym Pairs | Leveled-Up Literacy Learners<br>Words to Generate Antonyms |
|---|---|
| large/small | challenge |
| near/far | sorrow |
| laugh/cry | huge |
| scream/whisper | often |
| soft/hard | quietly |
| difficult/simple | worst |
| silent/loud | marvelous |
| wet/dry | above |
| lost/found | sweet |
| joy/sad | false |
| first/last | gently |

**Figure 2.5**

# 50 HANDS-ON ADVANCED Literacy Strategies

alongside the words. Leveled-up lit learners will be selecting an ant card and then each group member will take turns generating and sharing an antonym to that word with their small group. Begin this activity by modeling a game with students. Each child in the group will choose a specific color of ant from the game. Students will "jump" an ant from the Ants in the Pants™ game after they match [little lit] or generate [leveled-up] antonyms from their antonym ant cards. The player with the most of their "Ants in the Pants" is the winner.

## Hands-On Literacy Task

1. The students will play this game in groups of 2 to 4, each child choosing their own color of ant from the game. Students will work together to find the matching antonym ant cards [little lit], or they will randomly select an antonym ant card from the table and then take turns generating antonyms [leveled-up]. After matching or generating antonyms, students will "jump" their ant into the pants.
2. Continue playing the game until all the ant cards have been used. The player with the most "Ants in the Pants" is the winner.

## Whole Group or Small Group Reflection Prompt

"Choose one antonym ant card. Brainstorm a favorite antonym for that ant. Say or write a sentence with the word on the ant, then say the same sentence with the antonym you brainstormed. How does the meaning change?"

# ANTonym Ant Cards

Blackline Master 2.1

© Allison Bemiss, *50 Hands-On Advanced Literacy Strategies for Young Learners, PreK-Grade 2*. Routledge 2023

# 50 HANDS-ON ADVANCED Literacy Strategies

## 27 Mystery Box

### Skill

- ❏ Little lit learners: Synonyms/antonyms.
- ❏ Leveled-up lit learners: Synonyms/antonyms.

### Materials per Group

- ❏ Empty tissue box
- ❏ Various small objects for students to feel and describe*

*Connect this task to content area vocabulary by including objects that match units of study (i.e., if you are studying animals, include small figures of vertebrates and invertebrates). Then, as students are describing items, they can connect clues to the vocabulary they have been studying.

### Introduction

To prepare for this lesson, place a small object you would like students to practice generating descriptions of in the tissue box. Little lit learners can complete this activity together in small groups with an adult as an oral language task. The mystery box clue sheet would be optional or could be completed as an anchor chart with the adult scribing or annotating the students' ideas. Leveled-up lit learners can complete both the oral language and mystery box journal page. Model playing one round of this game for the students. For both levels, the students will take turns feeling the object, sharing a descriptive word, then a synonym and antonym for that word. Once each child has felt and described the object 2 or 3 times, the group can guess the object! You may want to have children generate one more description for their mystery box clue sheet now that they can see the object. If time permits, the teacher can give the group a different object, and the children can begin the game again.

### Hands-On Literacy Task

1. Students will work in groups of 2 to 4.
2. Each child will take turns feeling the object, choosing a word to describe the object, and generating synonyms and antonyms. Leveled-up lit learners can record their thinking on the mystery box clue sheet.

3   Once the group has generated 2–3 descriptions, they can guess the object and check to see if they were correct.
      *Optional: Students can generate one more journal entry after they can see the object. If time permits, repeat the activity with a new object.

## Whole Group or Small Group Reflection Prompt

"Most often we talk about what an object *is*, how does knowing what an object is *not* (or an antonym) help us identify an object?"

# MYSTERY BOX Clue Sheet

**ONE WORD TO DESCRIBE WHAT I FEEL.**
- ☐ 1ST TIME FEELING
- ☐ 2ND TIME FEELING
- ☐ 3RD TIME FEELING

**SYNONYM FOR MY DESCRIPTIVE WORD.**
- ☐ 1ST TIME FEELING
- ☐ 2ND TIME FEELING
- ☐ 3RD TIME FEELING

**ANTONYM FOR MY DESCIPTIVE WORD.**
- ☐ 1ST TIME FEELING
- ☐ 2ND TIME FEELING
- ☐ 3RD TIME FEELING

After you've given 2 or 3 descriptions, guess your item!

**Blackline Master 2.2**

# 28 Don't Spill the Beans

## Skill

- ❏ Little lit learners: Idioms.
- ❏ Leveled-up lit learners: Idioms.

## Materials per Group

- ❏ Don't Spill the Beans™ game
- ❏ Basket
- ❏ Beans idiom clue cards* (See Figure 2.6 for idiom list.)

## Introduction

Little lit learners and leveled-up lit learners will be working to understand the meaning of idioms and generate sentences with idioms. Choose the idioms you want your students to practice. Select as many or as few idioms as you would like students to explore. Write those onto the bean idiom clue cards. Then write the meaning of the idiom on the back. The youngest learners can do this as an oral language task in a small group with an adult. In the little lit version, students will take turns selecting a bean card from the basket. The adult (or reader in the group) will read the clue and meaning aloud from the bean card. The children will repeat the idiom and meaning after it is stated, adding a bean to the "bean pot" as they repeat it. Students then practice using the idiom in a sentence. After sharing a sentence, children will add a second bean into the bean pot. Leveled-up lit learners will play a similar version; however, the teacher (or child reading the clue cards) will *not* share the meaning of the idiom. Students will add a bean after guessing the idiom and then flip the bean card over to check their prediction. Then they will add a second bean when they each share a sentence using the idiom.

# 50 HANDS-ON ADVANCED Literacy Strategies

# DON'T SPILL THE BEANS IDIOM LIST

Use this list to create your "Bean Idiom Clue Cards". You can use as many or as few idiom beans as you would like for your students to explore. Write the idiom on the front and the meaning on the back of the card and then add them into your basket.

| Idiom | Meaning |
| --- | --- |
| let the cat out of the bag | to tell a secret |
| skate on thin ice | doing something risky or that may lead to trouble |
| raining cats and dogs | raining really hard |
| I'm all ears | ready to listen |
| cat's got your tongue | being unusually quiet |
| cost an arm and a leg | something is very expensive |
| change of heart | changing your thoughts or ideas |
| in hot water | in trouble |
| miss the boat | missed change or opportunity |
| hold your horses | pause or slow down |
| when pigs fly | something is unlikley to happen |
| put a bug in your ear | share an idea or thought with someone |
| snail's pace | moving slowly |
| cold feet | afraid or nervous before an event |

**Figure 2.6**

## Hands-On Literacy Task

1. The students will play this game in groups of 2 to 4. Students will take turns pulling a bean idiom card from the basket. Students will add a bean to the pot when they repeat the meaning of the idiom [little lit] or guess the meaning of the idiom [leveled-Up]. After checking the meaning, students can add a second bean to the pot when they generate a sentence using the idiom, so each child will add 2 beans to the pot for each new idiom.
2. The next student will have a turn pulling a bean card from the basket and the cycle will begin again. Students will continue playing until the beans spill from the pot.

## Whole Group or Small Group Reflection Prompt

"This game is called 'Don't Spill the Beans'! In this game, we literally spilled beans, but did you know the name also means "don't tell a secret." Share a sentence using "Don't Spill the Beans."

**Blackline Master 2.3**

© Allison Bemiss, *50 Hands-On Advanced Literacy Strategies for Young Learners, PreK-Grade 2*. Routledge 2023

# Part 2 Hands-On Language Comprehension

## 29 Morphology Tree

**Figure 2.7**

### Skill

- ❏ Little lit learners: Morphemes: base words and suffixes.
- ❏ Leveled-up lit learners: Morphemes: base word, prefixes, and suffixes.

### Materials per Group

- ❏ Small artificial tree
- ❏ Recording sheet [leveled-up lit learners]

# 50 HANDS-ON ADVANCED Literacy Strategies

- ❏ Clothespins (3 different colors representing *base word, prefix, suffix*)
- ❏ Morpheme sticky notes:
    a. Little lit: Write the following morphemes on its own sticky note: *base words*: play, help, stop; *suffix*: s, ed, ing.
    b. Leveled-up lit: Write the following morphemes on its own sticky note: *base words*: play, help, stop, watch; *prefix*: re, un; *suffix*: s, es, ed, able, ing, ful.

(*Use clothespins to attach each morpheme sticky note to the tree.)

## Introduction

Little lit learners will place a base word of their choice at the top of the tree. Students can then take turns adding suffixes to create new words and discuss how the meaning of each word changes as the suffix morpheme changes. If you are working with children who are not yet readers, you can adapt this to be an oral language activity by using pictures to represent the verb alongside the words. You can use the clothespins to represent the individual morphemes of the words you create. Leveled-up lit learners will create multiple words using the morpheme clothespins. Group together prefixes, suffixes, and base words. Students begin by clipping a base word to the top of the tree and then explore creating and recording words and meanings using various prefixes and suffixes. Prefixes will be placed on the left side of the tree, and suffixes will be placed to the right, creating a hands-on tree diagram.

## Hands-On Literacy Task

1. Students will work together in groups of 2 to 4, taking turns clipping a verb to the top of the tree and creating words using the morpheme clothespins by clipping them on the tree.
2. They will also discuss how the meaning changes as the morpheme changes. Leveled-up lit learners will also record words and meanings.

## Whole Group or Small Group Reflection Prompt

"Think of another word that uses the prefix (or suffix) _____. What does it mean? Challenge: Think of a word that you cannot add a prefix or a suffix to make a new word."

# MORPHOLOGY TREE
## Recording Page

| word sum | meaning | We created this word. |
|---|---|---|
| un + happy -> unhappy | ✗ 😊  un (not) happy (joy) -> sad | ☹️ unhappy |
|  |  |  |
|  |  |  |
|  |  |  |
|  |  |  |

**Blackline Master 2.4**

© Allison Bemiss, *50 Hands-On Advanced Literacy Strategies for Young Learners, PreK- Grade 2*. Routledge 2023

# 30 Syntax Salad

## Skill

- Little lit learners: Syntax.
- Leveled-up lit learners: Syntax.

## Materials per Group

- Syntax salad pieces (print on cardstock, color, laminate):
    a. Lettuce (who)
    b. Cheese (action)
    c. Tomato (when)
    d. Crouton (where)
    e. Dressing bottle (articles: the, a, an)
    f. Mushroom (blank)
- Bowl
- Dry erase marker

## Introduction

In this lesson, little lit learners and leveled-up lit learners will explore syntax by using the words in their salad bowl to create sentences. Print and laminate several of the salad pieces. Use a dry erase marker to write words for each category on the salad pieces and add salad pieces to the bowl. (See Figure 2.8.) The youngest little lit learners can create sentences using nouns (who) and verbs (action). Use pictures along with words to support children who are not yet independent readers. Students can use dry erase markers to add morphemes as needed (i.e., changing dog to dogs) and punctuation. Leveled-up lit learners can use the blank mushroom pieces to add adjectives and adverbs to expand their sentence. Model by thinking aloud as you create a "sentence salad." Share that each ingredient represents a different part of the sentence.

Part 2 Hands-On Language Comprehension

# SYNTAX SALAD WORD LIST

Use this list to create your "Syntax Salad Words". You can use as many or as few idiom words and categories as you would like for your students to explore. Laminate the salad pieces, then write the words in dry erase marker.

### Who (Lettuce)
dog
child
fish
cat
gorilla
wizard
lion
hippopotamus
snowman

### Action (Cheese)
read
sit
sing
dance
play
bake
clean
swim
hug

### When (Tomato)
ocean
school
market
zoo
stadium
park
library
studio
restaurant

### Where (Crouton)
Monday
last week
this morning
yesterday
tomorrow
next year
after school
all night
during lunch

### Articles (Dressing Bottle)
the
a
an

*Mushroom is left blank for students to expand the sentences they create with adjectives, adverbs or words of their choice.

**Figure 2.8**

## Hands-On Literacy Task

1. Students will work in groups of 2 to 4 creating a salad using the words provided in their salad bowl. *For the youngest learners, you can focus on noun (who) and verb (action) sentences.
2. Students work together to create as many sentences as possible. Children can use the blank mushroom pieces to expand their sentences by adding adjectives and adverbs. Use the dry erase marker to add punctuation and morphemes (i.e., *s* or *ed*) as needed.

## Whole Group or Small Group Reflection Prompt

"Pick one sentence and change the word order or punctuation. How does the meaning of the sentence change?"

# SYNTAX Salad

- Lettuce (Who)
- Cheese (Action)
- Tomato (When)
- Crouton (Where)
- Dressing Bottle (Articles)
- Mushroom (Blank)

**Blackline Master 2.5**

# 31 Prag-Meme-Tic

## Skill

- ❏ Little lit learners: Pragmatics.
- ❏ Leveled-up lit learners: Pragmatics.

## Materials per Group

- ❏ Silly animal meme emotion cards
- ❏ Meme template
- ❏ Pick a place sticks: craft sticks with the various locations:
  a. at recess with friends
  b. in school
  c. at an amusement park
  d. at home with your family

## Introduction

In this lesson, little lit learners and leveled-up lit learners will explore pragmatics by creating memes to compare what you may say in two different environments. Pragmatics is sometimes left out of the oral language and comprehension curriculum. You may need to explicitly explain the notion that we use different words, patterns, and inflection when we are at school than we do with our friends or family. Begin by modeling an example with students. Randomly select a silly animal meme emotion card and then randomly select two pick a place sticks. Think aloud with children as you share what you may say in one environment to another environment (i.e., confused – family: "What?! This doesn't make sense" vs in school: "I don't understand . . ."). Share that it's okay to use silly language or expressions when you are with friends or family but when you are in a serious environment your language should change. The youngest children can do this as an oral language task in small group with an adult, focusing on just one or two emotions or places at a time. Older little lit learners and leveled-up learners can capture their thoughts by writing the dialogue on the meme template provided.

## Hands-On Literacy Task

1. Students will work in groups of 2 to 4, taking turns pulling two locations to compare and one silly animal card. The children can then

brainstorm what they would say in each environment. Older children can capture their words on the meme template.
2. Students will continue this pattern, creating memes for as long as time permits.

## Whole Group or Small Group Reflection Prompt

"Look at your locations and memes. Are there any locations where you would speak similarly? Differently? Why do authors need to have a good understanding of pragmatics?"

| happy | angry |
| --- | --- |
| shocked | worried |
| annoyed | silly |
| sleepy | curious |

**Blackline Master 2.6**

© Allison Bemiss, *50 Hands-On Advanced Literacy Strategies for Young Learners, PreK-Grade 2*. Routledge 2023

# Prag-MEME-Tic Template

## Silly Animal Meme Card

| Environment 1 | Environment 2 |

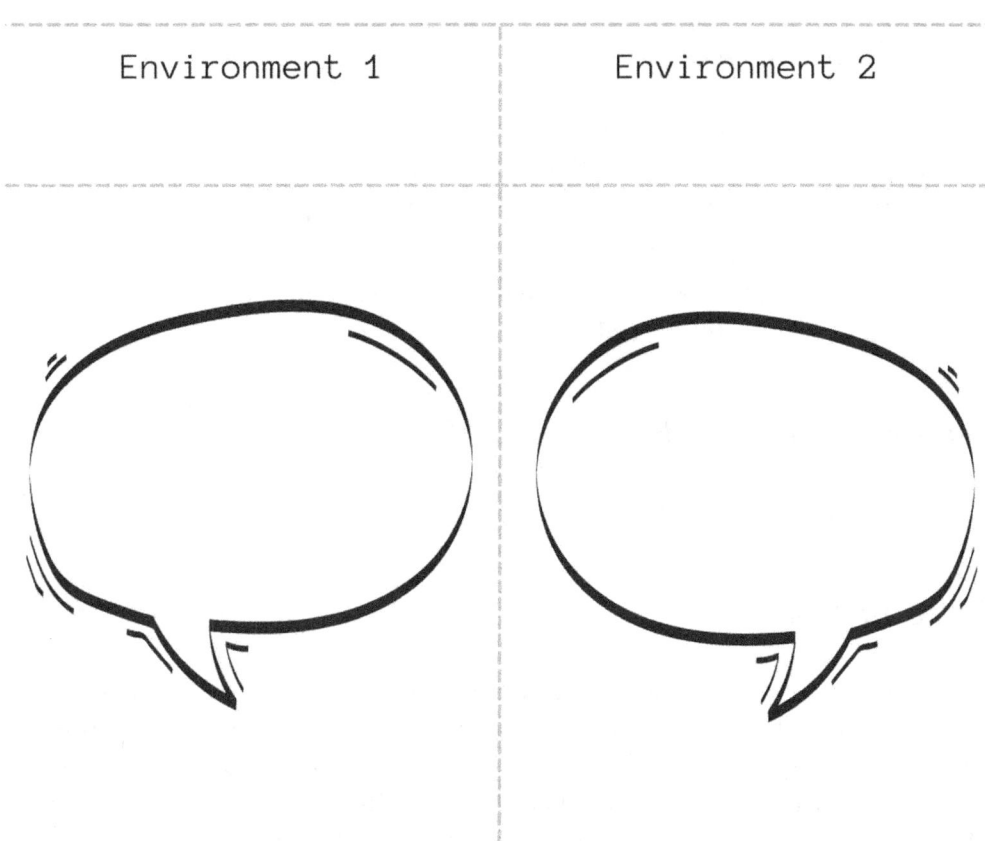

**Blackline Master 2.7**

© Allison Bemiss, *50 Hands-On Advanced Literacy Strategies for Young Learners, PreK-Grade 2.* Routledge 2023

## 32 Snack Time Sequencing

### Skill

- ❏ Little lit learners: Sequencing.
- ❏ Leveled-up lit learners: Sequencing.

### Materials per Group

- ❏ Snack time sequencing cards
- ❏ Tools: ¼ cup scoop, 1 gallon ziplock bag, 1 spoon
- ❏ Ingredients (pre-portioned and ready for groups to use):
    a. 1 cup berries of choice
    b. 1 cup of whipped cream or dairy-free alternative
    c. 4 chocolate or vanilla sandwich cookies

### Materials per Child

- ❏ 1 bowl, 1 napkin, 1 spoon

### Introduction

Little lit learners and leveled-up lit learners will explore sequencing a recipe. Little lit learners who are not yet readers can sequence the recipe using the pictures on the recipe cards while working in small group with an adult. Leveled-up lit learners can sequence the cards in small group and then have them checked by an adult before receiving ingredients. For a greater challenge with older children, you can omit the picture cards and show them the ingredients and tools. Then have the group write and sequence the directions as they invent their own recipe plan. Then give them the sequence cards to compare against the plan they brainstormed. Once the plan has been checked by an adult, they can receive their ingredients and create the snack using the plan they developed. Begin this task by showing students their ingredients and the direction cards. Model thinking aloud to show students how to order the steps by comparing two steps. Tip: For a faster paced lesson, pre-portion group ingredients to match the materials list and hand out on trays prepped for small groups.

### Hands-On Literacy Task

1. Students will work in groups of 4 sequencing recipe directions.
2. Once the teacher has checked the sequencing cards, students will receive their ingredients and create their snack time treat following the directions.

## Whole Group or Small Group Reflection Prompt

"Which steps can be switched in the recipe? Which steps cannot be moved around in the recipe?"

# Snack Time
## Sequencing Cards

| | |
|---|---|
| Gather your ingredients.    | Put 1/4 cup of berries in the bowl. |
| Gather your recipe materials.    | Top with 1/4 cup of whipped cream.  |
| Add cookies to zipper bag. Smash to make cookie crumbles. | Finish by adding 2 spoonfuls of crumbled cookies to the top!    |

**Blackline Master 2.8**

© Allison Bemiss, *50 Hands-On Advanced Literacy Strategies for Young Learners, PreK-Grade 2.* Routledge 2023

Part 2 Hands-On Language Comprehension

## 33 Graffiti Road

**Figure 2.9**

## Skill

- ❏ Little lit learners: Retelling/sequencing (visual prompts).
- ❏ Leveled-up lit learners: Retelling/summarizing.

## Materials per Group

- ❏ Black paper: cut in a rectangular strip to look like a road
- ❏ Toy car
- ❏ Nursery rhyme retelling graffiti cards [little lit learners]
- ❏ 3 small boxes covered in paper or brown paper bags to represent buildings

## Introduction

In this lesson, little lit learners will explore retelling and sequencing nursery rhymes using storytelling cards, and leveled-up lit learners will explore

# 50 HANDS-ON ADVANCED Literacy Strategies

summarizing a story through drawing and words. Both versions will ask students to think about the important events that occurred at the beginning, middle, or end of the story. Begin by modeling retelling a simple familiar story (i.e., "3 Little Pigs") by driving the car down the road, pausing at the beginning of the road to tell the beginning of the story, pausing at the middle of the road to tell the middle of the story, and then at the end of the road to tell the end of the story. Tell students you will be adding a twist to these story roads by adding graffiti art! Explain to students that artwork and words on the side of a building are sometimes called graffiti and the building owners have decided they'd like to hire an artist to help tell a story to the folks driving by. Show students the 3 paper-covered boxes or paper bags (buildings). Place one at the beginning of the road, middle, and end. Little lit learners will place their nursery rhyme storytelling cards in order by placing them up against the beginning, middle, or end buildings. Leveled-up lit learners choose a picture book or story of their choice to retell. They will use words and illustrations to tell the beginning, middle, and end of the story on each of the 3 boxes. Students place the boxes on the road in the correct order. Last, they drive the car along the road as they practice summarizing the story.

## Hands-On Literacy Task

1  Little lit learners will chant the nursery rhyme and then place their storytelling cards in order on their road. Leveled-up lit learners will read the story of their choice and then create graffiti to represent the beginning, middle, and end of the story on the 3 paper-covered boxes (buildings).
2  Each member of the group can take turns retelling the story down graffiti road.

## Whole Group or Small Group Reflection Prompt

"What is another story you'd love to retell using graffiti road? How would it look different?"

**Blackline Master 2.9**

# 34 Never Be a Know It All

## Skill

- ❏ Little lit learners: Questioning for understanding.
- ❏ Leveled-up lit learners: Questioning for understanding.

## Materials per Group

- ❏ Never be a know it all spinner
- ❏ Mentor text or storybook of choice
- ❏ Fidget Spinner (draw an arrow on one arm)

## Introduction

In this task, both little lit learners and leveled-up lit learners will explore questioning for understanding. Begin by choosing a book or text the small group or class has recently read. Introduce the idea that you can ask questions for two different purposes. You can ask questions for discussion, as in the following beach ball task, and you can also ask questions to better understand what you read or hear. Introduce and model generating "wh" questions about the mentor text you've chosen for the group. Then practice answering the questions together, thinking aloud as you generate the questions and sort through to find the answers. The youngest learners who are not yet readers will need to do this task as an oral language activity in a small group with an adult helping to model questions using the "wh" spinner. Older children can complete this task with an adult or independently in small groups. *Optional: You may want to intentionally model some questions that are not able to be answered using the text provided and then brainstorm other places to find information on the topic (i.e., other books, videos, online children's magazines).

## Hands-On Literacy Task

1. Students will work in groups of 2 to 4. Each group will have a common mentor text, book, or article to use to generate questions. Students will take turns spinning the fidget spinner, generating a "wh" question, and then working together to find the answer. If the answer cannot be found, they make a plan for where they could search for the answer.

2. Each member of the group can take turns spinning and generating a "wh" question and then working together as a group to find the answer within the mentor text or book of choice.

## Whole Group or Small Group Reflection Prompt

"We discussed many *wh* questions today, and now I want each of you to look back at your book and practice asking and answering a *how* question."

# NEVER BE A KNOW-IT-ALL!

- why
- when
- where
- what
- who

Draw an arrow on your fidget spinner and place it onto the center of the circle.

**Blackline Master 2.10**

## 35 Beach Ball Book Club

Figure 2.10

### Skill

- ❏ Little lit learners: Questioning for discussion/reflection.
- ❏ Leveled-up lit learners: Questioning for discussion/reflection.

### Materials per Group

- ❏ Classic beach ball (tricolor with 6 panels)
- ❏ Anchor text of choice

### Directions

Write one question or sentence stem on each panel of the beach ball (see Figure 2.10).

### Introduction

In this task, both little lit learners and leveled-up lit learners will explore questioning for discussion. Begin by choosing a book or text the small group or class

# 50 HANDS-ON ADVANCED Literacy Strategies

has recently read. Introduce the idea that you can ask questions for two different purposes. You can ask questions for understanding, like in the preceding "Never Be a Know It All" task, and you can also ask questions to discuss what you read or hear. Tell children that a book club is a group of people who read a book and then discuss the book together for fun. Today the beach ball will help guide the discussion! Model a quick game with our students. Have the children make an "L" on their left hand using their pointer finger and thumb. Whichever finger their left thumb (the one that makes the bottom of the capital L) lands on is the question they will answer as they catch the ball. Ask a child to toss you the beach ball and practice identifying the prompt on your left thumb. Then practice answering the questions together, listening, and connecting to the student's replies. The youngest learners will need to do this task as an oral language activity in a small group with an adult helping to model questions using the "Book Club Beach Ball" task. Older children can complete this task with an adult or independently in small groups.

## *Hands-On Literacy Task*

1. Students will work in groups of 2 to 4. Each group will have a common mentor text, book, or article to use to generate questions or responses.
2. Students will take turns tossing the beach ball responding to the questions or sentence stems on the beach ball, and discussing the topic together.
3. Continue playing this game for as long as time permits.

## *Whole Group or Small Group Reflection Prompt*

"We discussed many things about our book (or other text) using the beach ball today. How might discussing a book (or other text) with a friend help us understand the book?"

## 36 Class Connection Chain

### *Skill*

- ❑ Little lit learners: Making connections.
- ❑ Leveled-up lit learners: Making connections.

## Materials per Group

- ❏ Plastic multilink chain pieces or yarn
- ❏ Clothespins
- ❏ Paper
- ❏ Anchor text, media, or experience of choice

## Directions

Stretch the chain or yarn across the room to form the class connection chain.

## Introduction

In this task, both little lit learners and leveled-up lit learners will explore making connections to books, media, storytelling, or an anchor experience of your choice. Begin by reviewing the major events or key points of the book, media, or experience. Model making a connection to the anchor experience using the sentence stem "This reminds me of . . . ." Write and/or draw your connection on a piece of paper to model what the students will be creating. For leveled-up lit learners, model sorting your connection as either a text to self, text to text/media, or text to world connection. After sharing your connection, clip it to the class "connection chain" (or yarn string). Tell children they will create their own connection to the anchor book to add to the chain. The chain provides a visual representation for the schema of the class around a particular topic. *This is also a great way to reflect after a field trip.

## Hands-On Literacy Task

1. Students will work independently to draw and write their connections.
2. Then students will get into groups of 2 to 4 to share their connections to the anchor experience in small groups.
3. Each child will then clip their connection onto the "class connection chain."
4. Let children do a gallery walk along the completed chain to see all of the different experiences the class has that relate to the book or anchor experience.

### Whole Group or Small Group Reflection Prompt

"Which connections did you notice were similar/different as you looked at our class connection chain? How do our experiences help us better understand what we are reading, seeing, or hearing?"

## 37 Top Secret: Character Feelings Challenge

### Skill

- ❏ Little lit learners: Making inferences.
- ❏ Leveled-up lit learners: Making inferences.

### Materials per Group

- ❏ Manilla envelope labeled TOP SECRET
- ❏ Top secret clue cards
- ❏ Magnifying glass
- ❏ Anchor book of choice

### Directions

Find sentences or pictures in your anchor text that provide information on how a character feels. Write one clue on each detective card to help children make inferences about the character's emotion. (i.e., "Alex stamped his feet.") Place clues in Manilla TOP SECRET envelope.

### Introduction

In this task, both little lit learners and leveled-up lit learners will explore making inferences to determine a character's emotions by looking for clues from an anchor book of the teacher's choice. (This needs to be a book you've previously read with your students.) For the youngest learners, this can be done in small group as an oral language activity with a picture book, while older children can use either a picture book or a chapter book. Begin this lesson by modeling the task with your students. Introduce the anchor book to your students and review the different characters in the story and how their feelings or emotions changed throughout the story. Pull a clue from your Manilla envelope. Read the clue aloud to students. Get out your magnifying glass and find this part in the book. Share an inference for how the character is feeling in that part of the story and how the clue helped you determine the character's emotion.

## Hands-On Literacy Task

1. Students will work in groups of 2 to 4. They will take turns drawing a clue from the TOP SECRET envelope, read the clue, and use the magnifying glass to find that part of the story.
2. Students will take turns sharing their inference of how the character is feeling in that part of the story and how the clue helped them make that inference.
3. The children will continue this pattern until they've answered all of the clues.

## Whole Group or Small Group Reflection Prompt

"If you were writing a story about a character who was very happy, what clues could you give the reader with your words to *show* them the character was happy without *telling* them?"

# TOP SECRET Clue Cards

Blackline Master 2.11

# 38 Character Inside and Out

## Skill

- ❏ Little lit learners: Character traits.
- ❏ Leveled-up lit learners: Character traits.

## Materials per Group

- ❏ Character trait dice
- ❏ Anchor fiction book of choice

## Introduction

In this task, both little lit learners and leveled-up lit learners will explore examining character traits in a storybook or chapter book. Teachers can either select the book or allow students to bring their own book to small group. As with the previous lessons that required an anchor text, this should be a book the students have read previously or a book you've read together. Review that most characters in books have common categories you can explore.

How they:

- ❏ look
- ❏ feel
- ❏ think
- ❏ act/do
- ❏ say
- ❏ change

Introduce the character dice to the students and model a game for students. Take turns rolling the dice and discussing the character traits in the anchor text using prompts on the dice.

## Hands-On Literacy Task

1. Students will work in groups of 2 to 4.
2. Students will take turns rolling the dice and discussing the character traits for the character(s) in the story.

# 50 HANDS-ON ADVANCED Literacy Strategies

3   The children will continue this pattern until they've discussed each character trait prompts on the dice.

## Whole Group or Small Group Reflection Prompt

"Think of a character in a different book that shares some of the same traits as the character you discussed using your dice today and tell a friend about it."

# CHARACTER TRAIT DICE

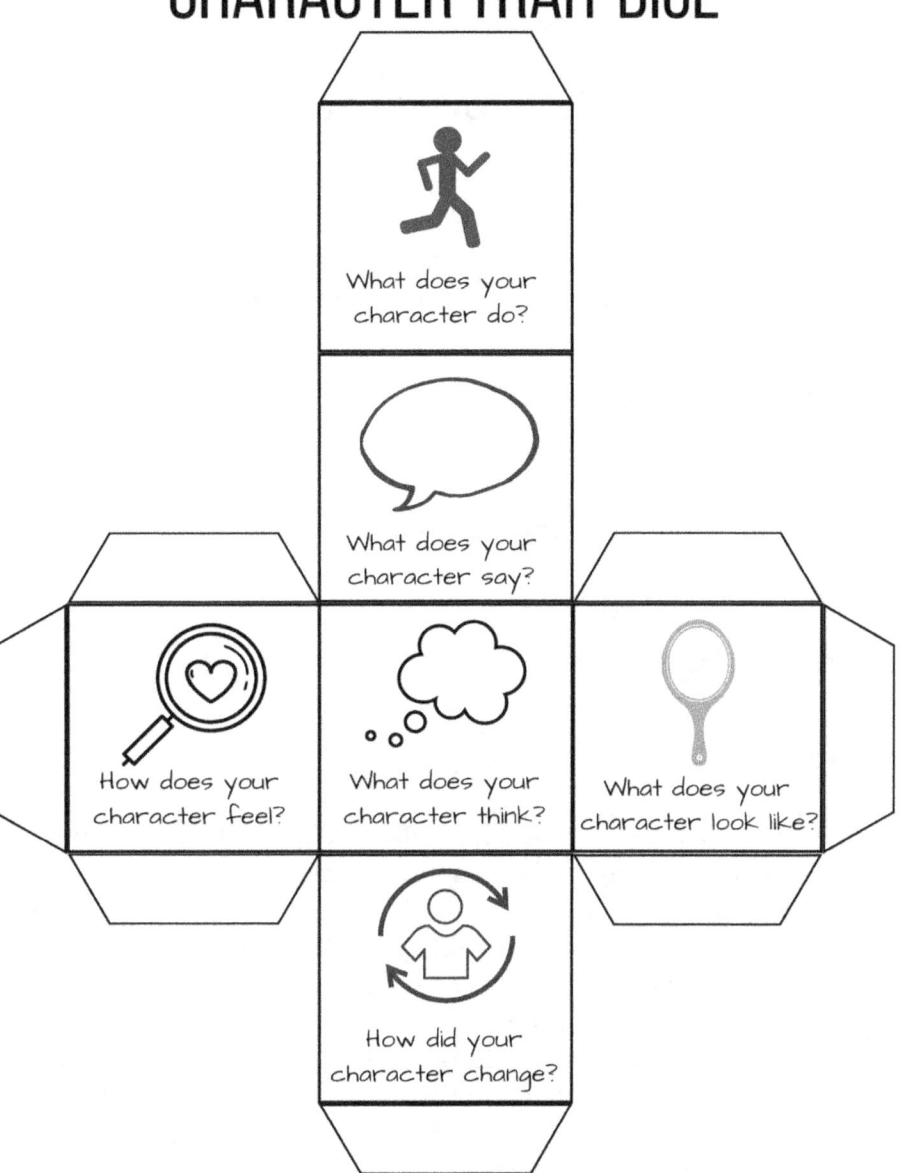

**Blackline Master 2.12**

© Allison Bemiss, *50 Hands-On Advanced Literacy Strategies for Young Learners, PreK–Grade 2*. Routledge 2023

# 50 HANDS-ON ADVANCED Literacy Strategies

## 39 Story Glove

### Skill

- ❏ Little lit learners: Characteristics of fiction: story elements.
- ❏ Leveled-up lit learners: Characteristics of fiction: story elements.

### Materials per Person

- ❏ Story glove:
    a. 5 hook and loop dot pairs or glue dots
    b. 1 glove
    c. Story element printables
- ❏ Anchor text of choice

### Introduction

In this lesson, little lit learners and leveled-up lit learners will determine story elements (character, setting, problem, solution, theme) in a book of their choice. The differentiation for this task will be reflected in the level of challenge in the fiction books the children use for the activity. Children who are not yet readers may choose a story that has been read aloud or a nursery rhyme/fairy tale they know well. Or you may choose to do this activity as a model experience analyzing a book together. Older children can choose a picture book or chapter book they have read previously to do this task. Students will work in pairs or in small group with an adult. Each child will begin by introducing their book. Then students will use the story glove to share their story with their partner or small group focusing on the story elements on the glove. Symbols have been included along with words to support beginning readers. *Optional singalong: Using the tune "Where is Thumbkin?", have children sing each story element category before they share that section of their book (i.e., Sing: Who are the characters? Who are the characters? Here they are. Here they are. The characters are ____ and ____. The characters are ____ and ____. Run away. Run away).

### Hands-On Literacy Task

1. Students will work in groups of 2 to 4. Students will introduce their book, sharing the title, author, and why they choose to share the book with the group.

2   Each child will take turns sharing the story elements using the fingers on their gloves one category at a time. For a fun twist have students sing along using the tune to "Where is Thumbkin?" to introduce each category of story element.

## Whole Group or Small Group Reflection Prompt

"How was your partner's book (or someone in your small group's book) similar to yours? How was it different?"

# Story Glove

Cut out these circles and use hook and loop dots or glue dots to attach them to each finger of the glove.

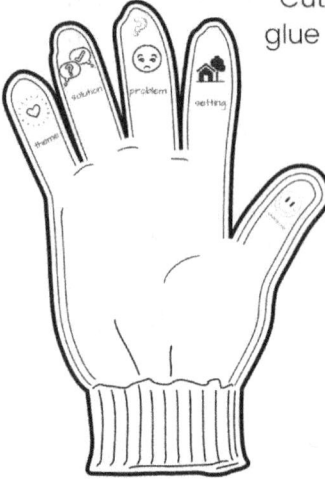   

## 🎵 Story Elements Song 🎵

Who are the characters, who are the characters? Here they are. Here they are.
The characters are _ and _ . The characters are _ and _. Run away. Run away.
Where is the setting, where is the setting. Here it is. Here it is.
The setting is _. The setting is _. Run away. Run away.
What is the problem, what is the problem? Here it is. Here it is.
The problem is _. The problem is _. Run away. Run away.
What is the solution, what is the solution? Here it is. Here it is.
The solution is _. The solution is _. run away. Run away.
What is the theme of the story, what is the theme of the story? Here it is. Here it is.
The theme of the story is _.. The theme of the story is _. Run away. Run away.

**Sing to tune of *Where is Thumbkin*.**

**Blackline Master 2.13**

# 40 Wild About Text Features

## Skill

- ❏ Little lit learners: Characteristics of nonfiction: text features.
- ❏ Leveled-up lit learners: Characteristics of nonfiction: text features

## Materials per Group

- ❏ Wild about nonfiction spinner printable
- ❏ Nonfiction article or book of choice
- ❏ Fidget Spinner (draw an arrow on one arm)

## Introduction

In this lesson, little lit learners and leveled-up lit learners will explore identifying and drawing meaning from various text features within a book of their choice. The differentiation for this task will be reflected in the level of challenge in the nonfiction books the children use for the activity. Begin by having students bring a nonfiction book of choice to small group. Model the task with your students. Spin for a text feature, then each person in the group will quickly look through their text to find that type of text feature, sharing what sort of information they learn from the text feature (i.e., Penguin diagram: Teaches us about the body parts of a penguin and how they help it survive). If your book doesn't have that category of text feature, you can brainstorm together how the author could have created one to go along with the topic of the book (i.e., No timeline in a book about gorillas, but the author could have created one to tell us about the different stages of a gorilla's development). As a fun challenge for older students, you may want to ask them to create this missing text feature. For the youngest learner, you can adapt this lesson to be done with one book in small group and you will think aloud together as you discuss the purpose of each text feature as you spin and search for them. Be sure to select a book that has an example of each of the text features you will be studying, since generating ideas for text features is more difficult than simply identifying them.

## Hands-On Literacy Task

1. Students will work in groups of 2 to 4. Students will introduce their book, sharing the title, author, and why they choose to share the book with the group.
2. Each child will take turns spinning a text feature. Then they will search through their text to find that text feature and share what sort of information they can learn from it. If their text does not have that text feature, the group can brainstorm how one could be created.

## Whole Group or Small Group Reflection Prompt

"Which text feature is your favorite (or least favorite) to use to learn new information? Why?"

# WILD ABOUT
## TEXT FEATURES SPINNER

| Map 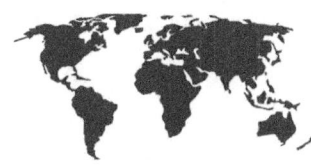 | Cutaway or Cross Section 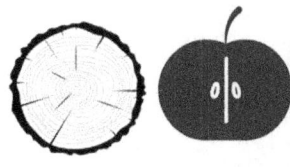 | Diagram with Labels 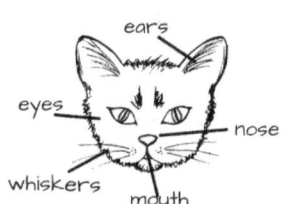 |
| --- | --- | --- |
| **Title,** Headings, or Subtitles | Draw an arrow on your fidget spinner and place it here. 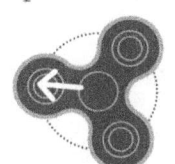 | Illustration  |
| Charts or Graphs 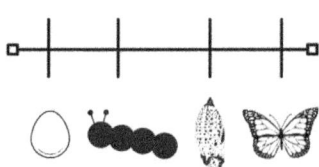 | Photograph  | Picture and Caption  A dolphin sleeps with one eye open. |

**Blackline Master 2.14**

## References

Mashburn, A. J., Justice, L. M., Downer, J. T., and Pianta, R. C. (2009). Peer effects on children's language achievement during pre-kindergarten. *Child Development, 80*(3), 686–702.

Shanahan, T. and Lonigan, C. J. (eds.). (2013). *Literacy in preschool and kindergarten children: The National Early Literacy Panel and beyond.* Baltimore: Brookes Publishing.

# PART 3

# Hands-On Writing

Although there are some writing connections scattered throughout the other parts of this book, it was important to intentionally include a section on encouraging children to practice various writing skills through engaging hands-on experiences. In this part, you will find 10 tasks for students reinforcing key writing skills.

We know writing takes years beginning with scribbles, lines, and drawings on a page and ending with novels, movie scripts, newspapers, emails, blogs, and all the other written communication forms we find ourselves surrounded by each day. Young children need a combination of play-based and explicit instruction in many different areas in order to learn to independently communicate their thoughts and ideas. They need fine motor practice to learn to shape the letters, word recognition strategies to be able to make the sound to letter transition into writing the words, rich oral language experiences to build the vocabulary they need to communicate ideas, and opportunities to explore comprehension and analysis strategies as a reader (i.e., sequencing a story or identifying figurative language) to then be able to apply those skills in their own writing (Hamby, Dunst, and Simkus, 2021). The literacy experiences in this section build on skills students have explored in the word recognition and comprehension sections of the book. For example one of the expository writing tasks in this book, "Snowman STEAM," builds on the skills students practiced in the comprehension section of the book called "Snack Time Sequencing."

DOI: 10.4324/9781003306627-4

The experiences shared in this section focus on skills within these categories including idea development (including oral storytelling) and drafting expository, descriptive, persuasive, and narrative writing; editing, and revision skills. While most tasks in this book can be done in short bursts of time, a few of the tasks in this section where students are engaging in idea development and drafting writing pieces will likely need to be divided up into several days of small group time to complete – depending on the age of the students you are serving. For example, if I am teaching the "Bear Share" task in this part, I will begin by reading the story and sequencing one day, then the following day I might introduce oral storytelling with the share bear. Then, on the final day, students could journal or draft a short story with their share bear. Could you choose to do this in one day instead? Absolutely! What about spreading it out over 5 days? Yes! The beauty of a supplemental resource like this book is you can easily adapt it to make it meet the unique needs of your little ones!

Speaking of adaptations, like the other sections of this book, specific suggestions for scaffolding are shared for various levels. If your *little literacy learners* are not yet independent writers, please don't skip this section! There are specific notes and suggestions on the most challenging tasks for how to adapt these experiences for very young learners. I lead monthly storytimes at our local public library and work with preschool teachers using these types of experiences on a regular basis. My general suggestions when working with our youngest learners are as follows:

- ❏ Use blank paper for them to draw/write as they share their ideas, responses, or stories.
- ❏ Have them share the ideas, or read their work to you or another as an oral language activity. Oral language and language comprehension skills help students learn to use their voice to share ideas that will eventually translate into their writing. (See Figure 3.1.)
- ❏ Scribe their words on a sticky note you can add to their work. This lets them know their words are important. It also allows you to display it so other adults who see the work later will be able to see their thoughts.

For young learners of all levels including *leveled-up literacy learners*, it's important to practice the peer conferencing, editing, and revision process so they can see that writing, much like science, is never really finished – there's always more to wonder, explore, and learn as you change your writing. This growth mindset is a thinking strategy to practice with all children.

This part also includes a couple of bonus sections! The first is a collection of 9 ideas for fine motor bins that you can keep readily available for students to use independently during center time or during times when you are working in

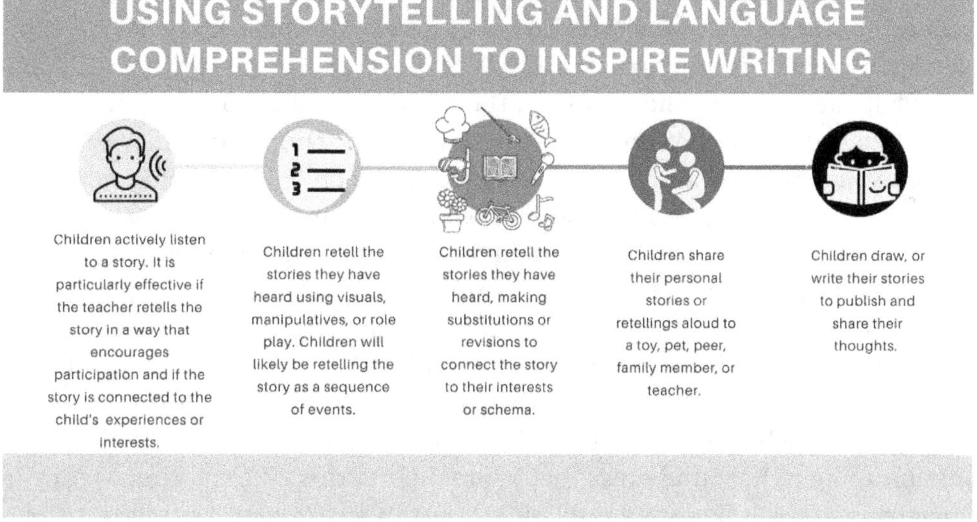

## USING STORYTELLING AND LANGUAGE COMPREHENSION TO INSPIRE WRITING

Children actively listen to a story. It is particularly effective if the teacher retells the story in a way that encourages participation and if the story is connected to the child's experiences or interests.

Children retell the stories they have heard using visuals, manipulatives, or role play. Children will likely be retelling the story as a sequence of events.

Children retell the stories they have heard, making substitutions or revisions to connect the story to their interests or schema.

Children share their personal stories or retellings aloud to a toy, pet, peer, family member, or teacher.

Children draw, or write their stories to publish and share their thoughts.

**Figure 3.1**

a small group with other students. Sometimes we assume if a child is advanced they will not need fine motor practice, but much like being gifted in mathematics doesn't mean the child is automatically gifted in art, it would be foolish to assume that a child gifted in literacy doesn't need fine motor practice. These bins also provide sensory support for children who may still be integrating those skills. If a child is excelling in fine motor skills, that is wonderful! You can up the level of challenge by introducing higher level vocabulary words to use along with the fine motor bins or you can introduce new engaging fine motor skills like cursive, calligraphy, or hand lettering as they explore words using the fine motor bins. In the beginning, you may choose to focus strictly on fine motor skills ("Five Essential Motor Skills for Handwriting Success," January 2022). If you are working with very young children who are not ready to write words, you can use these bins to work on a variety of prewriting skills like making different types of line. Later in the year, connect these bins to specific word recognition, comprehension or content area vocabulary students need to explore. An example of how to differentiate the "Play and Carve Bin": Pair it with an orthographic mapping task. Or have students explore vocabulary by carving synonyms or antonyms into the playdough. These bins can be prepared in advance and stored in a place where students can access them independently. Introduce one or two bins at a time in a small group. The sky is really the limit with these fun fine motor bins!

Writing is one important way for students to share ideas, but we know it's not the only way. There is a bonus section with 10 ideas for students to share ideas beyond writing. In this section, you'll find ways students can share using many different media forms. These ideas can be used on their own or paired with one of the tasks. In the "Shadow Zoo" task in this part, students are completing a journal on nocturnal animals. After students jot down their ideas and what they learn in their journal, they could turn that into a video report using Flipgrid or another age-appropriate video-sharing platform or they may brainstorm a plan for a pretend TV series with each episode being related to an interesting fact they learned about the animal they studied.

When was the last time you sent an email, took notes at a meeting, or texted a friend or family member? Those are things you've probably done in the last couple of hours . . . maybe the last couple of minutes. Writing and using their voice to share findings, thoughts, and ideas is something that will follow a child into adulthood. When working with advanced young learners we are building their schema, their foundation, with as many different experiences as possible to help them find areas that pique their curiosity. Exploring writing in engaging ways will build not only an interest in writing but positive attitudes and beliefs towards themselves as writers.

## 41 Share Bear: Be a Storyteller

### Skill

- Little lit learners: Storytelling and idea development.
- Leveled-up lit learners: Storytelling and idea development.

### Materials per Group

- *We're Going On a Bear Hunt* by Michael Rosen
- Bear hunt retelling cards

### Materials per Child

- 2 share bear templates (copied or traced onto cardstock and hole punched around edges)
- Yarn
- Cotton balls

### Directions

Cut out 2 bears from the template. Children can then color their bear, lace the sides most of the way, stuff the bear with cotton balls, and then finish lacing their bear.

## Introduction

Children will explore oral language, storytelling, and idea development. Read or sing "We're Going On A Bear Hunt." Invite students to retell the story using the cards. Show students your share bear, telling students anyone can be a storyteller just like the children in the story. Model storytelling to your share bear. You can share a big or small adventure like something you saw on your way to school. Invite each child to share an experience with the share bear and create their own share bear. Throughout the day or as a home–school connection, ask students to share moments with their share bear. Next, during writing, or center time, invite students to choose one story to draw or write in their journal. Although both levels are doing the same task, it offers natural opportunities for differentiation. Students will be expected to describe details, use vocabulary, and write or draw to match their unique level of readiness.

## Hands-On Literacy Task

1. Students will work in small groups with the teacher, reading and retelling *We're Going On a Bear Hunt*. The teacher and students will take turns storytelling to the share bear.
2. Students will then create and take home their own share bears to practice sharing.
3. Students choose one story shared with the bear to draw or write in their journal.

## Whole Group or Small Group Reflection Prompt

"How might authors use events in their daily life to inspire writing (fiction or nonfiction)?"

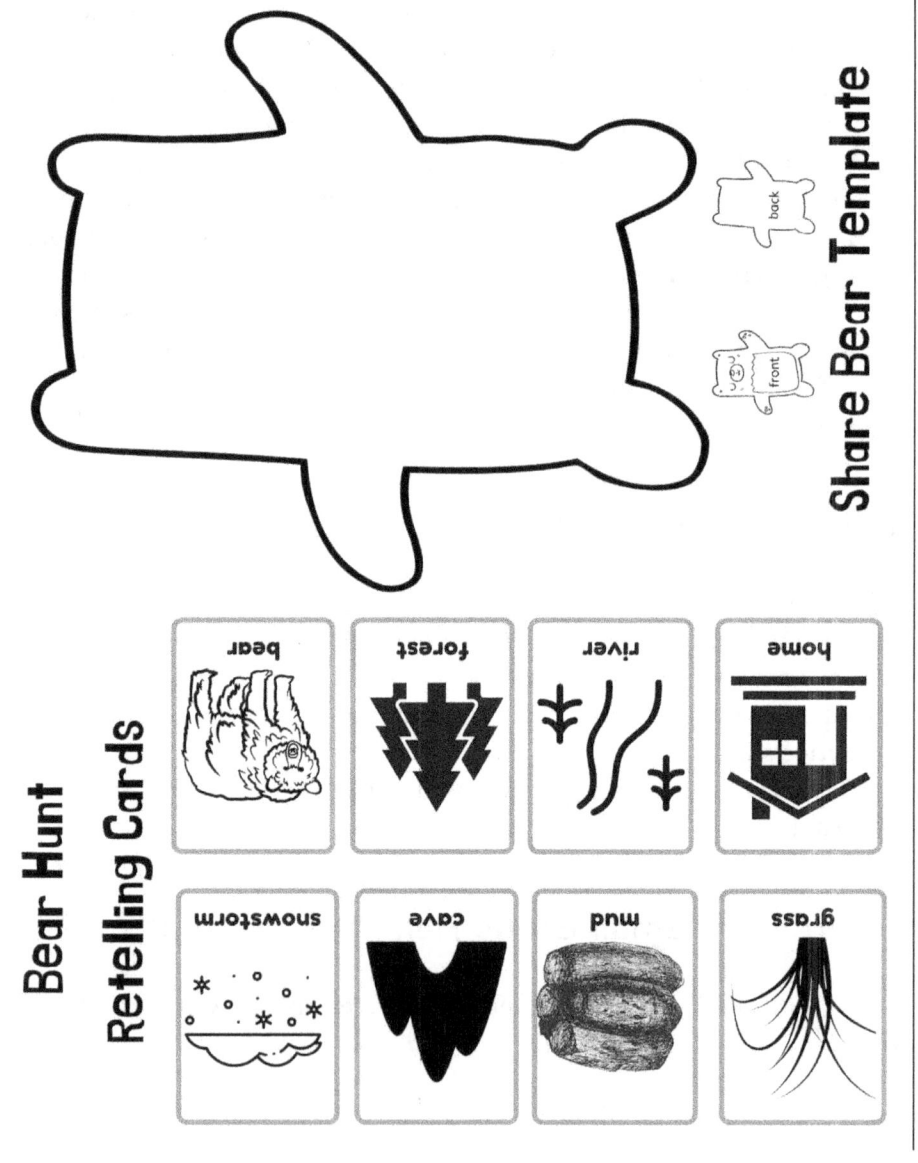

Blackline Master 3.1

# 42 Beary Delicious Details

## Skill

- ❏ Little lit learners: Descriptive writing: sensory details.
- ❏ Leveled-up lit learners: Descriptive writing: sensory details and figurative language.

## Materials per Child

- ❏ Gummy Bears
- ❏ Beary delicious details organizer

## Introduction

In this task, students will explore how noticing and describing experiences using details from their five senses can strengthen their descriptive writing. Begin by reviewing the five senses and then model the activity with students so they understand how to complete the graphic organizer. The youngest little lit learners can complete this task in small group with an adult as an oral language task first. The adult can use the organizer as an anchor chart to record each group member's descriptions. Then students can draw and write letter strings to communicate their individual descriptions. For beginning writers, it is a perfect opportunity to practice adding details to two word sentences (i.e., Jamie ate. → Jamie ate a sweet red Gummy Bear.) Leveled-up lit learners can write their descriptions in pairs or independently. Challenge them to include similes, metaphors, alliteration, personification, or other figurative language examples in their descriptions. If students are just beginning to learn about figurative language, introduce one strategy at a time. However, if your students have already had experience exploring these tools, give them the opportunity to choose any figurative language device they'd like to use.

## Hands-On Literacy Task

1. Students will work independently or in pairs for this task. Students will explore the Gummy Bears using all five senses.
2. Students will record their descriptions on the graphic organizer. Young learners can do this as an oral language task in small group with a teacher creating an anchor chart of their sensory descriptions. They

can then practice using the details to write sentences. Older children can do this independently or in small group. Challenge them to add figurative language details into their descriptions.

## Whole Group or Small Group Reflection Prompt

"How do sensory details help writers paint a picture in the reader's mind? How does this help the reader better understand the writing?"

# Beary Delicious Details

## SENSORY WORDS

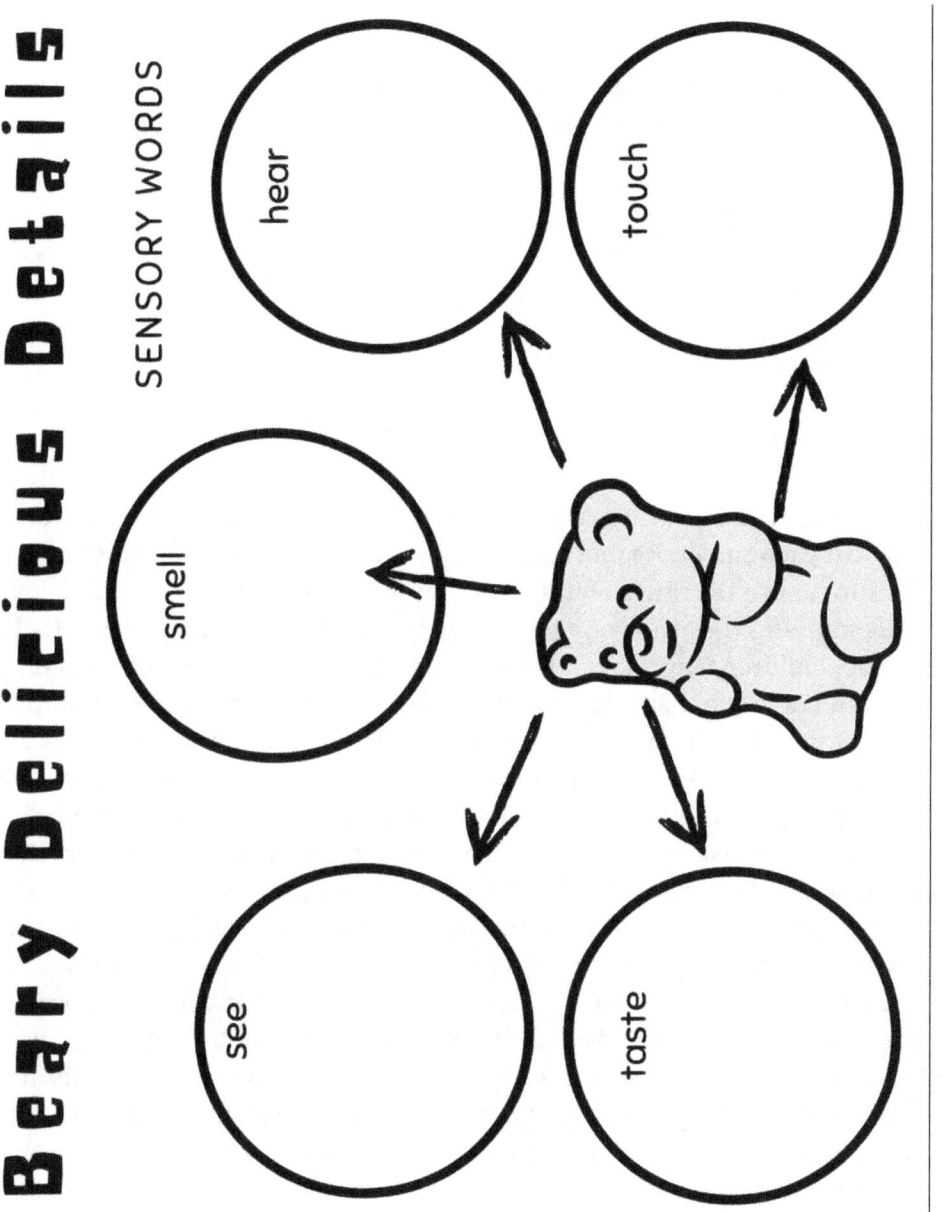

## 43 Number Narrative

### Skill

- ❏ Little lit learners: Narrative.
- ❏ Leveled-up lit learners: Narrative.

### Materials per Child

- ❏ 2 to 4 Wikki Stix™
- ❏ Journal or blank paper

### Introduction

In this lesson, little lit learners and leveled-up lit learners will explore narrative writing using a number. Begin this lesson by modeling number narrative writing. Be sure to use the range of numbers that is appropriate for the child's level of understanding (i.e., the youngest learners may focus on numbers 1 to 10, while older children may use greater numbers). Use your Wikki Stix™ to create a few numbers that are special to you. Introduce the notion that *all* numbers tell a story (i.e., 1 – the number of pets I have; 18 – the number of years I've been teaching; 15 – the number of states I've visited). Invite children to work in pairs, taking turns building a number and telling the story of that number orally. They will reuse Wikki Stix™ each time they create a new number. Then ask students to choose one number they created and tell that story in greater detail. Have them build the number on the top of the page and then draw and/or write to tell the story of their number. This quick write can later be used to revise and turn into a personal narrative if you choose. It is also a great way to have students introduce themselves to you or other students at the beginning of the school year. For the youngest learners, you can adapt this to be building numbers on a tens frame using circle stickers and a tens frame. Children who are not yet ready for lined paper can use a blank sheet of paper to draw and write their number narrative.

### Hands-On Literacy Task

1. Students will work in groups of 2 to 4, taking turns building numbers using their Wikki Stix™ and telling their unique story that goes along with that number.

2   Students will choose one number to do a quick write about and tell the story of the number they chose.

## Whole Group or Small Group Reflection Prompt

"Why is it important to remember that all numbers tell stories?"

# 44 Mystery Text

## Skill

- ❏ Little lit learners: Narrative.
- ❏ Leveled-up lit learners: Narrative.

## Materials per Pair

- ❏ Mystery text screenshot cards (cut apart phones and laminate)
- ❏ Texting journal and brainstorm sheet

## Introduction

Begin this task by discussing texting, explaining how it is a form of written communication. However, at times technology glitches and we only see part of the message. Share the images and/conversation fragments on the mystery text cards. Little lit learners and leveled-up lit learners will use the mystery text cards (pictures or text) to think creatively and write a narrative that explains the rest of the story. Little lit learners who are not yet able to write independently can use blank paper to draw and write letter strings. Then they can orally tell you the story they've made up to go along with the picture or text fragment. Older little lit and leveled-up lit learners can use the texting journal to write the rest of the story. Model this activity for students by choosing one image or text from the mystery text cards, and brainstorm answers to *wh* questions: *who, what, when, where, why* to create the story. *If your students have already done the "Never Be a Know It All" task from the comprehension section you can connect to that story analysis experience to help them understand how to use *wh* questions for writing. This activity can extend into the oral language skill of pragmatics if you discuss with children how the audience of the text will change the tone of voice (i.e., the words you would use to text your principal would likely be different than what you would text to your friend).

# 50 HANDS-ON ADVANCED Literacy Strategies

### Hands-On Literacy Task

1. Students will work independently or in pairs to choose one of the mystery text cards.
2. Students will brainstorm in pairs using *wh* questions: *who, what, when, where,* or *why* to create the story, or narrative, to explain the mystery text.
3. Students will draw and or write to tell the story they've created for the mystery text.
4. Allow students to share their mystery text stories with the class or allow them to do a walk around the room to take a look at other students' writing/drawings.

## Whole Group or Small Group Reflection Prompt

"I noticed several students chose the same picture or text, but their stories are all different. Why do you think we can look at the same picture or words and each come up with a unique story?"

**Phone 1:** Can you believe my dog did that?

**Phone 2:** So... long story short, I'm going to buy a new one right now.

**Phone 3:** That is why I'll never use a jump rope again.

**Blackline Master 3.3**

# Texting Mystery Brainstorm

sketch the story here

What
How
Who
Where

---

# Texting Journal

Blackline Master 3.4

# 45 Would You Rather?

## Skill

- ❏ Little lit learners: Persuasive.
- ❏ Leveled-up lit learners: Persuasive.

## Materials per Group

- ❏ Would you rather? choice cards
- ❏ Empty tissue box (would you rather? box)
- ❏ Would you rather? journal page

## Directions

Color, laminate, and cut apart would you rather? choice cards and place in the box.

## Introduction

In this task, students will use silly questions as the hook for an engaging opinion writing brainstorm session. Students will explore supporting their opinions with reasoning. To prepare for this task, you may need to first introduce or review facts and opinions with students. Little lit learners and leveled-up lit learners can play this game in pairs or in small groups. First, the group will randomly draw one card from the would you rather? box. Students will discuss which option they would choose, orally providing two reasons why they made that selection. The students will take turns drawing 3 to 4 cards, discussing each one in the same manner. After students have discussed 3 to 4 cards, each child will choose one to write about on the journal page provided. Young children who are not yet independent writers can complete this activity together in pairs or small group with an adult as an oral language task and then draw pictures on blank paper to support their reasoning. An adult can annotate their words onto the drawing or on a sticky note as they share their persuasive writing.

## Hands-On Literacy Task

1. Students will work in groups of 2 to 4.

2. The group members will take turns pulling a card from the would you rather? box. Students will discuss their opinion providing two reasons for their choice.
3. Once the group members have had the opportunity to discuss 3 to 4 cards, students will choose their favorite question to write about using the journal page provided. *See adaptation note for young learners.
4. Students can share their journal entries, and/or drawings, in small group.

## Whole Group or Small Group Reflection Prompt

"How did you use facts to support your opinion? Why are our opinions different? Is it okay to be different?"

**Blackline Master 3.5**

# Would You Rather
## Opinion Writing

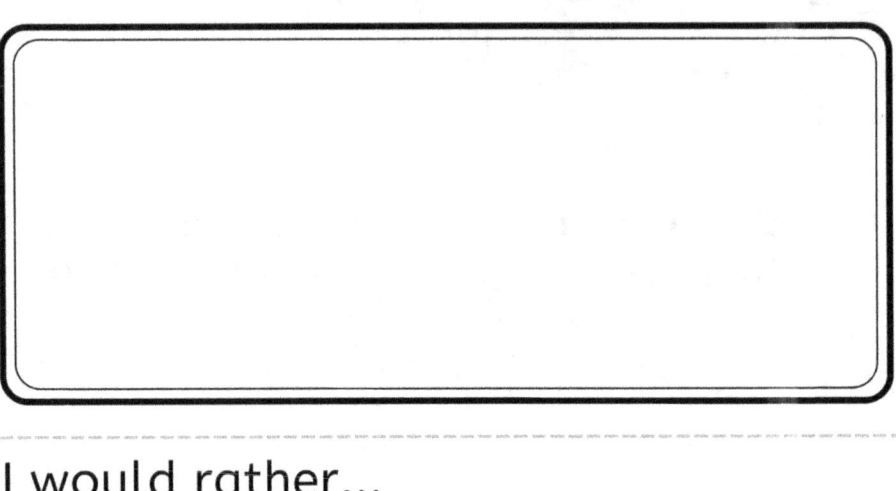

I would rather...

Reason 1 | Reason 2

**Blackline Master 3.6**

## 46 Shadow Zoo

### Skill

- ❏ Little lit learners: Expository.
- ❏ Leveled-up lit learners: Expository.

### Materials per Group

- ❏ Shadow zoo poem and shadow puppets
- ❏ Wooden sticks or straws
- ❏ Flashlight
- ❏ Nighttime zoologist report
- ❏ Nonfiction text and/or media matching shadow puppet animals

### Directions

Cut out shadow animals and tape them onto wooden sticks or straws.

### Introduction

Begin this lesson by gathering age-appropriate media and texts on the nocturnal animals matching the shadow puppets you choose to use for the task. (If you have a local conservation park or wildlife refuge, it would be a great time to invite them in or set up a video meeting for small groups to practice interviewing an expert.) In this experience, little lit and leveled-up lit learners will explore brainstorming, questioning, determining importance, and expository writing. Set up a flashlight per small group pointing toward the ceiling or wall. Sing the "Shadow Zoo" to the tune of "Twinkle, Twinkle Little Star," allowing students to choose shadow puppets to explore. Let the small groups sing the song a few times as they explore and play with different animals. Turn on the lights, ask students to choose an animal they are curious about. Students can document their research on the nighttime zoologist report journal page. Determine the guidelines for how you want students to document what they've learned (i.e., little lit learners may find 6 interesting facts to share or create 6 pictures with captions while Leveled-up lit learners will be responsible for asking and answering 6 research questions or creating 6 different text features on their animals). Tailor this page to match the unique needs and interests of your students. Young learners can draw or write the research on blank paper.

# 50 HANDS-ON ADVANCED Literacy Strategies

### Hands-On Literacy Task

1. Students work in groups as they chant or sing the poem while exploring with the puppets.
2. The children will choose one animal to study and use the zoologist report page to capture their notes or drawings as they look through books and media.

### Whole Group or Small Group Reflection Prompt

"Now that you've learned all about this nocturnal animal, how might you share it with others?"

## Shadow Zoo

Shadows, shadows
On my wall
Animals, animals
Big and small
Dancing, dancing
In my light
Playing, playing
Through the night
Shadows, shadows
On my wall
Animals animals
Love them all

**Blackline Master 3.7**

**Blackline Master 3.8**

## 47 Snowman STEAM: How To

### Skill

- ❏ Little lit learners: Expository.
- ❏ Leveled-up lit learners: Expository.

### Materials per Group

- ❏ 4 biodegradable packing peanuts
    - a   Orange marker (draw triangle nose) and black marker (draw circle eyes and buttons)
- ❏ Bowl of water and spoon
- ❏ Snowman steam: how to cards
- ❏ Snowman steam: planning page

### Introduction

Little lit and leveled-up lit learners will be exploring writing an expository piece to teach others how to do a steam investigation. Ask students what happens to snowmen when they get warm? They melt! Tell the children you will be working with pretend snowmen today. Since you don't have a heat source you can't melt them, but you can make them disappear. Ask students to think about a time when they've seen something seem to disappear without heat (i.e., cookie in milk). Tell students the goal for today is to explore with their snowman (show a biodegradable packing peanut) to learn what the word *dissolve* means. This lesson is similar to the "Snack Time Sequence" comprehension task. Students will sequence the snowman steam picture cards. Next, give students the snowman steam planning page and have them write or draw how they plan to dissolve their snowman. For little lit learners, consider writing sentence stems on the planning page to guide them. The youngest children should work in small group, sequencing and orally sharing the directions. Annotate their thoughts on an anchor chart to capture their plan. For leveled-up lit learners, begin by showing students the materials. Invite them to brainstorm the steps before sharing the cards. Students check with the sequencing cards before writing their plans. Students will complete the investigation following their plan.

### Hands-On Literacy Task

1. The students will work in groups of 2 to 4 to sequence snowman steam cards.
2. Then they will write a snowman steam plan for how to complete the investigation.
3. Finally, they will complete the steam investigation using the directions they created.

### Whole Group or Small Group Reflection Prompt

"Were you able to follow your snowman steam planning page directions? What changes would you make before sharing it with other friends who may like to try this task?"

# SNOWMAN STEAM CHALLENGE

| | |
|---|---|
| Gather your materials.  | Put 1 cup of water in the bowl.   |
| Put the snowman in the water.   | Stir for one minute. 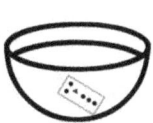  |
| Pour the water and dissolved snowman down the sink.  | Use a towel to clean up any spilled water or mess.  |

**Blackline Master 3.9**

# Snowman STEAM Plan

**Goal:**

**MATERIALS NEEDED:**

**FIRST**

**THEN**

**FINALLY**

**CLEAN UP NOTES**

Turn the page over to add drawings or diagrams.

**Blackline Master 3.10**

## 48 Lights, Camera, Action!

### Skill

- ❏ Little lit learners: Types of sentence/writing convention/fluency.
- ❏ Leveled-up lit learners: Types of sentence/writing convention/fluency.

### Materials per Group

- ❏ 5 to 10 sentence strips (see intro for how to choose sentences)
- ❏ Punctuation (types of sentences) microphone template
- ❏ 4 cardboard tubes or toilet paper rolls

### Directions

Choose 5 to 10 sentences from a mentor text or write your own that are at the appropriate level of challenge for your students to explore various ending punctuation and write them onto sentence strips. Glue punctuation (types of sentence) microphones onto cardboard tubes.

*If leveled-up lit learners are ready to move beyond exploring ending punctuation, create punctuation microphones with parentheses, commas, colons, semicolons, or hyphens.

### Introduction

Begin by reviewing the 4 types of sentence (declarative, imperative, interrogative, exclamatory). Tell the students today they will be actors and practice reading lines with various punctuation. Model a game. Invite 4 students to play, each holding a punctuation microphone. Let each child take turns reading the sentence using their punctuation microphone, discussing how meaning changes (i.e., Elijah ate it? vs. Elijah ate it!). Little lit learners who are just beginning to learn about ending punctuation can compare reading 2 at a time rather than all 4. The youngest little learners can do this with 2- or 3-word sentences and can complete it as an oral language activity. Leveled-up lit learners can help write the sentences they will use in the game. To increase the challenge further you can also adapt this activity to explore other types of convention such as parentheses, commas, colons, semicolons, or hyphens.

# 50 HANDS-ON ADVANCED Literacy Strategies

### Hands-On Literacy Task

1. Students will work in groups of 4 with each child holding a punctuation microphone.
2. Turn the sentence strips face down, then the group chooses one at random and each child takes a turn reading the sentence with their punctuation microphone into the microphone like an actor. Students discuss how the meaning changes with punctuation and sentence.

### Whole Group or Small Group Reflection Prompt

"How does punctuation change the meaning of the sentence?"

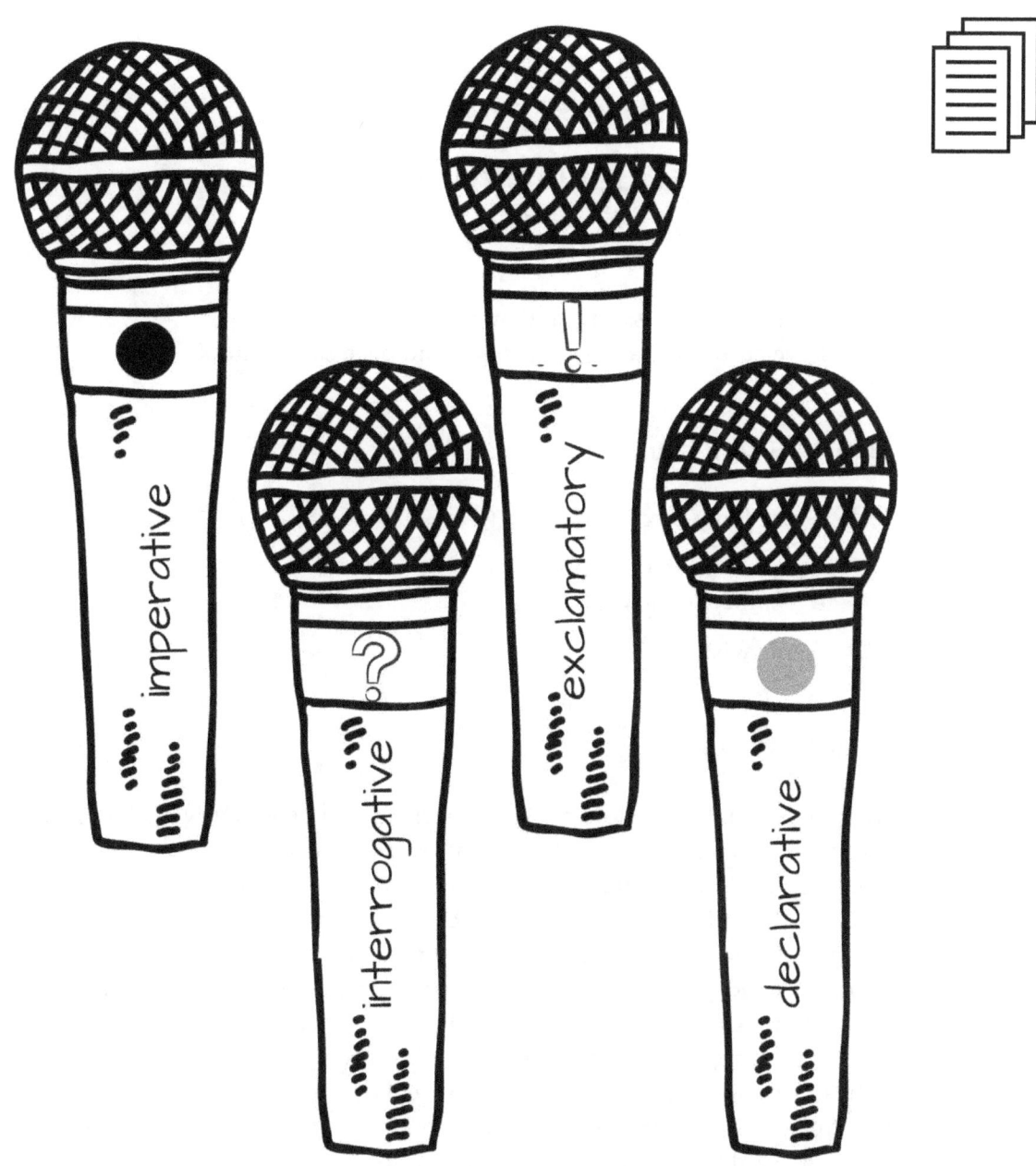

**Blackline Master 3.11**

© Allison Bemiss, *50 Hands-On Advanced Literacy Strategies for Young Learners, PreK-Grade 2*. Routledge 2023

# 49 Genie Writing Wishes

## Skill

- ❏ Little lit learners: Revision and peer conferences.
- ❏ Leveled-up lit learners: Revision and peer conferences.

## Materials per Pair

- ❏ Genie lamp box:
    - a   genie lamp template
    - b   empty tissue box
- ❏ Genie wish cards

## Introduction

In this task, little lit and leveled-up lit learners will explore revising a piece of their own writing in partners. Begin introducing the idea of revision and peer conferencing. An engaging connection to introduce peer conferencing here is to use the "Friend Like Me" song from Disney's *Aladdin.* Discuss that sharing writing with friends can help make our writing stronger and that is what you will practice today with the genie game today. There are two types of wish card students will explore today. One is to "wish" for the other students in the group to tell something specific that worked well in the writing. The second type of "wish" is for a specific type of revision. Model this task for children by sharing a short piece of your own writing. Rub the genie lamp and pull out a revision wish card. Read your "wish" card aloud and discuss it with the class. Students will play the genie revision game the same way, except each child in the pair will read their writing. They will respond to one other's writing for each wish card they pull. Students may want to make notes on their work as they listen to one another's comments. The youngest learners can work in pairs alongside an adult and complete this task using their writing/drawings as an oral language activity. Create a wish card with a star to represent sharing a positive, then create 2 cards with specific skills for revision (i.e., a card with colors to represent adding color details).

### Hands-On Literacy Task

1. Students will work in pairs. Each child will begin by sharing their writing.
2. One child will pull a wish card. Each child will respond to their partner's card prompt.
3. Students will continue taking turns pulling wish cards for as long as time permits. Students may want to make notes on their writing as they discuss wish cards.

### Whole Group or Small Group Reflection Prompt

"What is one positive your partner shared about your writing? How might you add more of that strength to your piece?"

# Genie Writing Wishes
## Lamp Template

One thing you did really well I want to try in my writing is...

I loved...

I thought this part was really ___ (i.e. funny, silly, clever)

I'd love to see a text feature or figurative language in this part...

I'm wondering if there is a part you'd like to think about together?

I'd love to hear a bit more about...

**Blackline Master 3.12**

© Allison Bemiss, *50 Hands-On Advanced Literacy Strategies for Young Learners, PreK–Grade 2*. Routledge 2023

## 50 Editor Spinner

### *Skill*

- ❏ Little lit learners: Editing.
- ❏ Leveled-up lit learners: Editing.

### *Materials per Pair*

- ❏ Editor spinner
- ❏ Fidget spinner (draw an arrow on one arm of the fidget spinner.)

### *Introduction*

In this task, little lit and leveled-up lit learners will explore editing their own writing using the editor spinner. Begin by modeling the activity with your students to be sure they understand the task on each section of the spinner. Give the spinner a whirl and see where it lands. Next, you and your buddy will take turns reading through each of your pieces and finding a place in the writing to edit using the editor spinner's task. After you've completed the first task, let the partner have a turn spinning and you will repeat the process with the new task. If the spinner lands on the same task, you can find a second spot to change or you can spin again. Tip: It is helpful if the teacher's writing piece used to model the task is not yet polished and contains errors similar to what you typically see occurring in your students' writing. As with the "Genie Wish" revision task, the youngest learners can work in pairs alongside an adult and complete this task as an oral language activity. If the editor spinner includes tasks that are too advanced for the learner, create your own editor spinner with 1 or 2 items the students can use to revise their drawings or writings (i.e., add a curvy line to your drawing or practice writing the first letter of the first word of your story). For young learners, it is okay if the skills on the spinner you create are different than what you typically think of as editing, you are introducing students to the idea that their work can be changed and adapted.

### *Hands-On Literacy Task*

1. The students will play this game in pairs.
2. The first child will spin the editor spinner then both children will take turns reading through their writing and finding a spot in their piece

to do the editing task. Students can work together to find the place to make the change or they can work independently and share their changes with their buddy after they note it on their work.
3. After students have shared their changes, the second child will spin to find a new task. Students will repeat this process until they've made several changes to their writing.

## Whole Group or Small Group Reflection Prompt

"Why is it important to read through our work with others and make edits before publishing?"

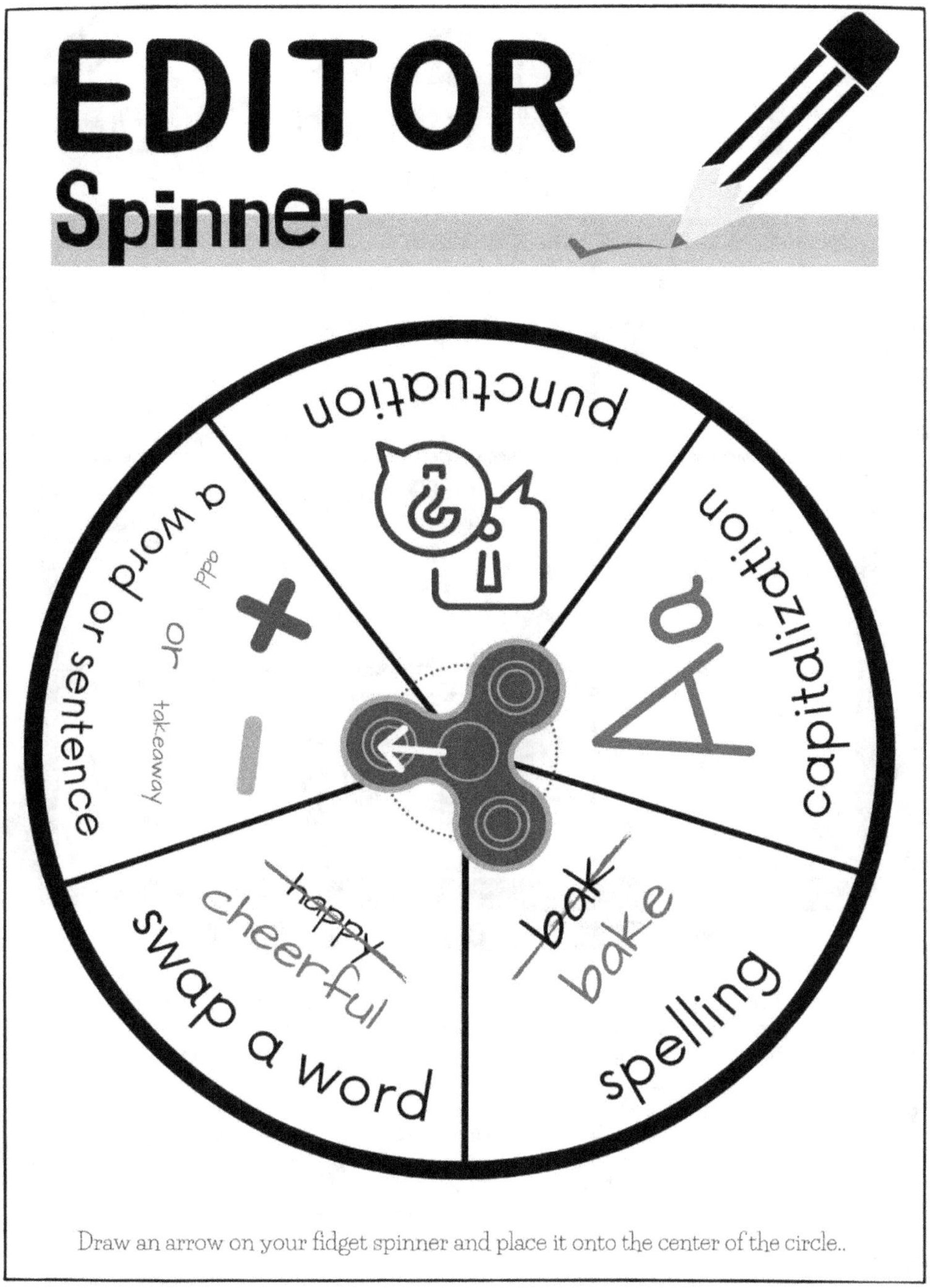

# EDITOR Spinner

Spinner sections: punctuation, capitalization, spelling, swap a word, add a word or sentence (+ or − takeaway)

Draw an arrow on your fidget spinner and place it onto the center of the circle..

**Blackline Master 3.13**

## BONUS
# FINE MOTOR FUN
### Bins for Littles

| Bend It Bin | Play & Carve Bin | Sand Tray Bin |
| Squishy Bin | Build It Bin | Tweeze It Bin |
| Road Map Bin | Rainbow Bin | Jewel It Bin |

## MATERIALS LIST

- Bend It Bin: Pipe Cleaners or Wikki Stix™ and Parchment Paper
- Play and Carve Bin: Playdough and Wooden Stick or Other Carving Tool
- Sand Tray Bin: Meal Prep Box with Sand, Salt, Sprinkles or Sequins
- Squishy Bin: Gallon Zipper Bag with Hair Gel and Food Coloring
- Loose Parts Bin: Loose Parts and Felt Sheet
- Tweeze It Bin: Tweezers and Cotton puffs
- Road Map Bin: Lines, Letters or Words on Sentence Strips and Toy Car
- Rainbow Bin: White Crayon and Watercolor Paint
- Jewel It Bin: Glue and Plastic Jewels or Beads

**Figure 3.2**

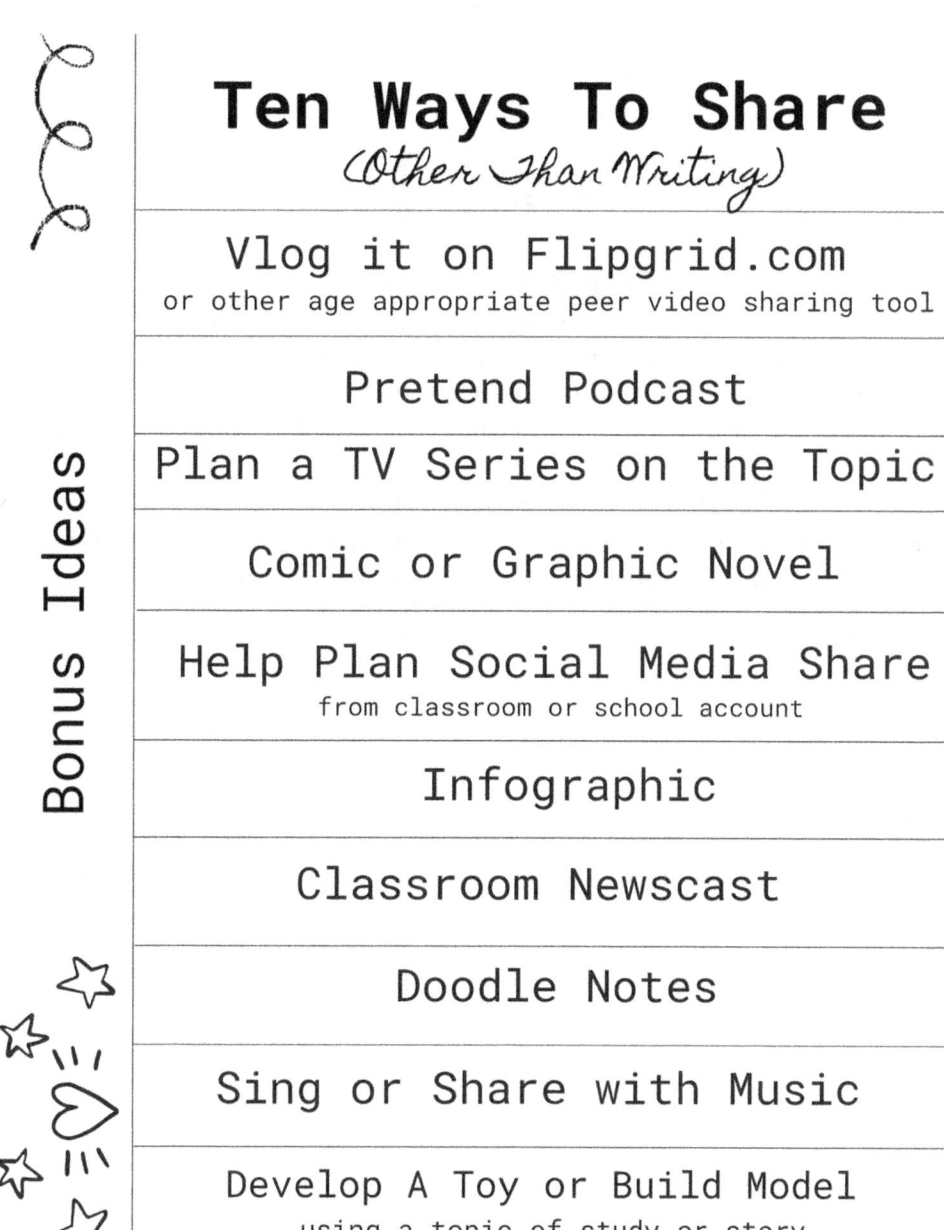

**Figure 3.3**

# References

Five Essential Motor Skills for Handwriting Success. (January 2022). Griffin Occupational Therapy. https://www.griffinot.com/motor-skills-for-handwriting/#:~:text=Gross%20and%20fine%20motor%20skills,a%20child%27s%20readiness%20to%20write.&text=Next%2C%20the%20children%20develop%20dexterity,with%20Duplo%2C%20bricks%20and%20beads

Hamby, D. W., Dunst, C. J., and Simkus, A. (2021). Children's story retelling as a literacy and language enhancement strategy. *CELLReview*, 5(2), 1–14. http://www.earlyliteracylearning.org/cellreviews/cellreviews_v5_n2.pdf

For Product Safety Concerns and Information please contact our EU representative GPSR@taylorandfrancis.com
Taylor & Francis Verlag GmbH, Kaufingerstraße 24, 80331 München, Germany

www.ingramcontent.com/pod-product-compliance
Lightning Source LLC
Chambersburg PA
CBHW080938300426
44115CB00017B/2861